Bad Theology

Bad Theology

Oppression in the Name of God

Leah Robinson

scm press

© Leah Robinson 2023

Published in 2023 by SCM Press
Editorial office
3rd Floor, Invicta House,
108–114 Golden Lane,
London EC1Y 0TG, UK
www.scmpress.co.uk

SCM Press is an imprint of Hymns Ancient & Modern Ltd
(a registered charity)

Hymns Ancient & Modern® is a registered trademark of
Hymns Ancient & Modern Ltd
13A Hellesdon Park Road, Norwich,
Norfolk NR6 5DR, UK

British Library Cataloguing in Publication data

A catalogue record for this book is available
from the British Library

ISBN 978-0-334-06105-2

Typeset by Regent Typesetting
Printed and bound in Great Britain by
CPI Group (UK) Ltd

Contents

Acknowledgements

First, this book is dedicated to my loving and constantly supportive husband, Stuart Gibb – as well as our feline zoo: Salem, Kylo, Zero and Beethoven.

In addition, my thanks go to all the people of Charlotte who have supported and encouraged me in this – Good Books and Drinks girls, especially.

Also, to Kristy Whaley, who offered friendship and an unhinged passion for systematic theology, which was vital for checking my work in this book. We make a well-rounded – if not terrifying – team.

Finally, this book is dedicated to all those who have suffered from bad theology. It may not erase your experiences, but I hope you can see that God does not belong exclusively to the people who harmed you.

I stand with you.

PART I

Introduction

It is 2009, and I am sitting in a very dark, intimidating bar in Belfast. I am a Practical Theology PhD student at the University of Edinburgh and I have come to Northern Ireland to research the theology of reconciliation in the context of this beautiful and complicated country. While I have been doing my field research here, I have managed to meet a wide variety of people, mostly peacebuilders, working tirelessly to establish some sense of stability in their home country. In this instance, however, I am meeting with someone who has been described to me as a 'community officer'. Not in any official sense, I was told, but someone who 'looked after' a community in a non-official capacity. I had already come into contact with people like this, as Northern Ireland's divisions mean that neither side especially trusts the police to protect them. This particular community officer has heard that I have been out and about in the neighbourhood asking people questions. He wants to meet and chat, and the invitation makes it quite clear that I have little choice in the matter.

As I sit waiting in the bar for the officer, I find myself suddenly surrounded by a large entourage. The officer sits down next to me and offers a hand. I introduce myself as a researcher, as a minister and as someone interested in theology. The room visibly relaxes. If I am a minister then I am not on 'the other side'. My officer proceeds to spend the next hour and a half telling me about his own personal theology. He does not openly admit to killing anyone, but he hints. And as he expounds upon his understanding of the Bible, his belief system, his favourite theologians, I realize that this man has an incredibly complex and well-thought-out theological understanding. This is not someone who has simply strung together various biblical texts to confirm his actions. He is not quoting paramilitary rhetoric. He is quoting well-respected theologians. In fact, he could have been transplanted into a research seminar at any higher education institution. But, instead, he is discussing how his faith confirmed his actions, which included: violence, prejudice and perhaps murder.

It is not a new idea that religion and violence are connected. Both at Edinburgh and in my current position at Pfeiffer University in the USA, I teach a class called 'Religion, Violence, and Peacebuilding', which examines how religion has influenced both practices of violence and peace. I am currently writing a chapter for the upcoming *Wiley-Blackwell Companion to Religion and Peace*, but at the same time I am actively referring to the *Blackwell Companion to Religion and Violence* for this book. A common theme within these texts is the word 'religion'. The perspective on religion and violence or peacebuilding is viewed through a historical or sociological lens. So when scholars speak of religion as violent, it is from studying various instances in which those claiming a certain religion have acted in a way that results in some form of violence. The criteria for this type of violence to be seen as religious varies, but in general there are connections between the violence and a sacred text, or an interpretation of the text, or a religious community/leader's influence on a particular person, or some specific event against a group that has led them to take up arms against another group.

In some ways this is much easier than the task at hand. One can easily see the connection between interpretations of certain texts and violent acts. Or leadership in certain religious contexts causing followers to commit terrible actions. Or some event in history that has led to other events that lead to violence justified by religion. These events in history can be marked and examined. What is different in these scenarios is that they are stated as being anomalies within religious traditions. Those violent actions that are justified by religious beliefs are discredited as not really being religious at all. I find this a most unhelpful argument – the reason being that this type of understanding of religion distances religious interpretations from violent acts. And while people of a certain religion may want their religion distanced from any and all negative actions, this is simply not realistic. One may not think that a certain religious person within a tradition is acting according to what they consider the normative, interpretative behaviour of that religion, but it does not make that person any less a part of the religion. This type of logic is no longer talking about what makes a person this religion or that – instead we now talk about whether a person within a religious tradition has come to the right or wrong interpretative conclusion in accordance with that religion's belief system.

My interest in this subject is just this. As opposed to exploring the connection between religion and violence in a way that is sociological or ethnographical, I'm using this book to look at these events theologically. This makes the task far more difficult. The assumption is that theology is 'God knowledge', and the presumption in this is that people are somehow capable of attaining knowledge about God. I believe this to be painfully egotistical. While theologians are actively looking for knowledge about God on earth, the idea that we are somehow receiving a direct line of communication about the state of the world from the Almighty does not feel realistic. And if we are, then there are some serious contradictions in these dialogues.

This book will reflect my views in this way, and it will base itself on the assumption that theology is a human activity. Being a human activity means that theology is filtered through the wants, desires and beliefs (among other things) of those who are doing the interpreting. As a result, there can oftentimes be theological conclusions that look a lot like a human desire as opposed to something related to divinity. These desires can reflect the motivations of those who are interpreting. Accordingly, my question in this project relates to these motivations and their consequences: What if the motivations of human interpretation are so overpowering that the practice of theology is used as a means of oppression, as opposed to a divine desire for human flourishing? In other words, how does one speak of Practical Theology as something that is a motivation for extreme violence and oppression?

The fields of systematic, historical and philosophical theology have long strived to locate and collate ideas related to the divine. They have also looked to take these themes and create understandable resources for use within theological colleges and ministry. While these areas are important to Practical Theology, scholars in this field have been far more interested in what happens to these resources once they are enacted and, perhaps more importantly, translated in the world. The how, what, why and where of theology is the core of the discipline.[1] As a result, the field of Practical Theology has long offered an opportunity for researchers to analyse theology from a qualitative point of view.[2]

My book is literature-based, or theory-based, but also engages with examples from the social world in a way that highlights the impact of context on theology. Practical Theologians have long embraced Robert Schreiter's and Stephen Bevans's view that theology is contextual. As Bevans asserts: 'All theology is contextual theology.'[3] Specifically, he argues that contextual theology is Practical Theology. This is an idea that will serve as a central theological claim within this book. To say that motivations for genocide such as Hitler's is Practical Theology is a bold claim that some will push back against. However, when viewed through the lens of the fact that all theology is contextual, and a human construct, and that Hitler proclaimed his actions as God-ordained, at some point one must come to the conclusion that there might just be bad Practical Theology out there. This Practical Theology most certainly does not come from God, but it fits into the criteria of what is considered theology (in the descriptive sense, not the divine sense).

My argument is that Christians throughout the world must recognize that theology can be contextually corrupted. Theology is a human endeavour as well as a God-given gift. However, sometimes the tilt in theological interpretations (and consequent actions based on that theology) are more about the human context and what a person believes God *is* saying than what God is saying in the world. This book argues this viewpoint through chapters that look to define the field of Practical Theology (as far as that is possible); the human construction of God as a practical theological task; and how that construction can lead to 'good' and 'bad' Practical Theology. With all of this theory/theology in hand, we will look to examples of this bad Practical Theology in practice. I could have included many more chapters on this theme, but I am approaching only the topics that I have experienced in my own research. I will leave the unenviable task of exploring further examples of bad Practical Theology to those who come after me. That being said, I do hope that I have opened the conversation up for this type of research to occur, as well as offered criteria by which other scholars can discuss good and bad Practical Theology.

Of course, there are difficulties in claiming that there are examples of oppressive Practical Theology, or indeed just plain bad theology. It requires that I situate myself on a side of what is good or bad, which is an uncomfortable situation for any Practical Theologian who does qualitative research. I know that through my examples my personal context will emerge, and I am at peace with that. As Bevans articulated, all theology is contextual, and so I would not expect my analysis of theology to be anything but from my own point of view. That being said, I do not want to speak to some theological echo chamber, and I hope the examples used in this book will be agreed upon by some, if not many, and that they will maintain a compelling argument throughout. My principal foundation underlying this book is that Practical Theology is both the *action* of human construction as well as the *product* of human construction. As a result, it is overwhelmingly possible that both the product and the action of Practical Theology can be oppressive – principally because of the human nature of theology in general. Practical Theology is not written in an eschatological utopia. It is written in the very real, very concrete, very oppressive world in which we live. This world has influenced theology through-out time, and continues to influence it today. This influence is not always life-affirming. It is often life-denying, and it is the duty of the Practical Theologian to be able to discern when a life-denying stance is being taken – even if it is being taken within one's own theological circle.

The danger in this is obvious. The idea of a theological witch-hunt is very real (and very historical). The task of Prac-tical Theologians is not to deem what is heretical and what is orthodox. We leave that to the denominational bodies and the systematic theologians. It is our responsibility to have the tools to be able to see when theology has been *produced* or *acted out* in such a way that it has led to oppression. Often this acknow-ledgement occurs many years after the oppression took place. But to have the knowledge that such events occur, and all in the name of theology, serves the Practical Theologian in their continued endeavours to create a more just world.

Finally, I have been asked why I need to write a book like this. Further, why a book on something so negative? As I sit writing this in 2022, I am very aware that we are currently going through a global shift in politics and religion (among other things). We have been through a pandemic; economics are shifting; and tides are rising. As I look at the rhetoric that surrounds me with regard to issues like theology and race, gender, sexuality, immigration or economics, I find myself less shocked and instead more reminded of theology that I have heard or read already. Some of this bad Practical Theology in 2022 is theology we have encountered before. If we can learn to recognize it as such, and openly name it as such, then it is possible that we might be able to be a source of liberation in this world. Not just with regard to oppression, but with regard to theology itself. A theological friend of this project, Gordon Kaufman, offers similar ideas and beliefs about this type of research and its importance:

It is right and proper, therefore, that theologians and others should be continually engaged in examining and re-examining received ideas of God, that we criticize those ideas as sharply as we can in terms of the actual functions they perform in human life, and that we reconstruct those ideas so they will serve more adequately as vehicles of our fuller humanization.[4]

Is this re-examining of theology in the hope of naming and learning from bad Practical Theology idealistic? Perhaps. But I am a Practical Theologian, and idealism is the plain in which we most thrive. So with an ounce of grace, a little bit of faith, and perhaps an overwhelming sense of hope for the future of theology ... Let us continue.

Leah Robinson
Charlotte, North Carolina, USA
August 2022

Notes

1 Richard Osmer, *Practical Theology: An Introduction* (Grand Rapids, MI: William B. Eerdmans, 2008), p. 4.

2 One such text is John Swinton and Harriet Mowat, *Practical Theology and Qualitative Research* (London: SCM Press, 2006). The most recent text about research in Practical Theology is Zoë Bennett, Elaine Graham, Stephen Pattison and Heather Walton's *Invitation to Research in Practical Theology* (Abingdon: Routledge, 2018).

3 Stephen Bevans, 'Contextual Theology as Practical Theology' in *Opening the Field of Practical Theology*, ed. Kathleen A. Cahalan and Gordon S. Mikoski (Lanham, MD: Rowman & Littlefield, 2014), p. 45.

4 Gordon Kaufman, *The Theological Imagination* (Louisville, KY: Westminster John Knox Press, 1981), p. 264.

I

Setting the Scene: Practical Theology as my Methodology

However, the failure to encounter, explore, and be challenged by realities that expose the messy, risky, dangerous, horrific, and wonderful elements of our world is a highly problematic way to avoid or protect ourselves ... Our production of theology, then, is as much 'lived theology', constituted by the messiness of life, as is the lived faith and theology of those we consider ordinary believers.[1]

Practical Theology as the theology of the church

It is a tradition with every book published in the field of Practical Theology that there is a requirement that a thorough repeating of the history of our own field must occur (trust me, just look it up!). This exercise is a result, in many ways, of our academic area having a less than stellar record of defining itself. You do not see systematic theologians or historical theologians giving readers the complete history of their existence before ploughing into the topic at hand. However, Practical Theologians time and again will refer back to their history in order to say what we, indeed, are.

The reasoning behind such historical regurgitation is a result of Practical Theology feeling as though it must define itself in relation to other theological disciplines. While I push back against the continuous stream of reliving Practical Theology's history, I will offer a brief history that directly relates to the project at hand.

Why do we have such a fascination with naming our forebears in the field of Practical Theology? Since Schleiermacher's work in this field, the discipline of Practical Theology has attempted to define itself, or in some cases to deny that definition is even possible. Either way, Practical Theology has on the one hand been praised for its fluidity and on the other hand dismissed as a subject without foundation. Eric Stoddart, who is a Practical Theologian at the University of St Andrews, offers the following:

> Practical Theology is sometimes dismissed as lacking in intellectual rigour, and I wonder if it is our reluctance as Practical Theologians to be obsessed with 'definitions' that accounts for much of others' disdain. Not being able to produce a definitive definition of 'Practical Theology' is only one manifestation of this rebellious streak. Practical Theologians understand power. Particularly the power to name.[2]

The irony of the resistance to naming is not lost on those of us who study Practical Theology. From our beginnings in the academic study of the discipline, we were aware of the power struggles that naming can entail. Our own naming began in grandeur, specifically our accepting of the designation of 'Crown of the Theological Disciplines'[3] that was offered to us by the German theologian Friedrich Schleiermacher. As a theologian wrestling with the implications of the Enlightenment on subjects that were ambiguous at best, Schleiermacher desired to place theology within the realm of subjects that were seen as legitimate in this new context. His answer to the Enlightenment question was Practical Theology. According to Schleiermacher, the answer to theology being a scientific subject was the fact that theology was a human endeavour that could be observed and recorded. According to Tice, Schleiermacher saw theology as not only a 'human enterprise' but also 'a reflection on God's presence with humanity'.[4] And while the influence of God's presence on the theological conclusions of humanity was vital, the most important aspect of Practical

Theology was the understanding that people could never be taken out of the theological equation. Humans were the crafters of the dogmas and doctrines that were taken to be divine truth by the church. While it would be possible to dismiss theology in this humanistic light, Schleiermacher saw the importance of the stabilizing nature of using common doctrines as a framework for the church at a given time. He also felt it was important for students of theology to be able to identify theological norms in the church no matter how human and contextual they might be.

Following on from the idea of the church being held up by the framework that common doctrines provided, another key aspect of Schleiermacher's viewpoint was the importance of understanding theology as historical. In his *Brief Outline of Theology*, Schleiermacher offers the following: 'Each student of theology must form one's own clear historical vision for oneself, concerning both information about the total career of Christianity and information about the moment of history in which one lives.'[5] Schleiermacher is focused on the training of ministers in these statements, but his thoughts on the historicity of theology are important to the development of Practical Theology as an academic discipline. He is urging students to understand that their adherence to a theological dogma or doctrine came from a place in history. This does not mean that the student cannot follow a particular belief as divinely inspired, but it does mean that they should know that it was 'issued from someone else'[6] and accordingly each student must come to their own conclusions about theological issues with this in mind.

Schleiermacher's contribution to the field of Practical Theology cannot be overstated. He was advanced in his understanding of the influence of the Enlightenment on subjects such as theology. As a result, he attempted to find a reasonable means by which theology could be viewed in relation to the progress of society at this time. His view of theology as an inspired human endeavour that was historical in nature has been vital to the way that Practical Theology has developed in academia, especially in relation to how the subject utilizes the social sciences to study theology. Schleiermacher knew the importance of having dogmas in the church in order to keep the institution going, but he also knew that these beliefs needed to be examined with a critical eye. His focus, however, was firmly on the context of ministry, and the field of Practical Theology would remain in the world of the church for many years to come. Even with the developments of the pastoral theologians in the twentieth century, Practical Theology was still seen as something ministers did. It was this way until the work of Don Browning brought the subject outside of the walls of the church, and into the secular world at large.

Practical Theology as beyond the church

Don Browning was Alexander Campbell Professor of Emeritus of Ethics and the Social Sciences at the Divinity School, University of Chicago. Browning takes the ideas put forward by Schleiermacher and expands the discipline into a more secular world outside of strictly ministerial studies. He acknowledges that there have been several recent developments in the world of theology that can be seen as being practical in nature – namely, political theology and liberation theology. He embraces these new developments as practical approaches and offers a theoretical means by which Practical Theology might continue to develop as an academic discipline.

Browning is quick to state that Practical Theology has been seen as a less important discipline in theological institutions in comparison to other theological areas.[7] He offers the following: 'The field of Practical Theology has been throughout its history the most beleaguered and despised of the theological disciplines ... To admit that one is a practical theologian invites even deeper skepticism.'[8] Browning believes that the time for viewing Practical Theology in this way is over. He recognizes that there is a rebirth time for Practical Theology in the contemporary world. He acknowledges the primacy of philosophy and theory in many areas of academic studies, including theology itself, but says that the developments of recent years have meant that practice has been brought to the forefront in theological analysis.

According to Browning, the reasoning behind this rebirth lies in the fact that theology has, perhaps erroneously, been seen as a direct interpretation of God's ideas. This view was most prominently proposed by the theologian Karl Barth. Browning states that, in Barth's view, theology was practical only in so much as God's revelation (in its pure form) was applied to situations at a given time. Browning pushes back against this view: 'There was no role for human understanding, action, or practice in the construal of God's self-disclosure ... The theologian moves from revelation to the human from theory to practice, and from revealed knowledge to application.'[9] Browning states that many theologians see Barth's view as at least partially wrong, because it does not take into account the historical nature of theology. In his view, however, Barth is at least partially right. To further elaborate, Browning offers an additional aspect of the theory to action framework. He proposes a view whereby theory influences practice and, as a result, practice influences theory. According to Browning, Barth believed that the theological community should rid itself of its tendencies to justify ideas based on cognitive reasoning. Instead, they should accept completely theology as being inspired by God and revealed through the text. Browning believes that this is an impossibility when it comes to humanity. All theology has hints of humanity attached to it, according to Browning, because humanity will always want to add, remove or adapt theological ideas that are presented to them.

Browning's argument is that theology is, fundamentally, a Practical Theology. According to him, abstracting theology does not make theology any more legitimate in theological institutions or elsewhere. Instead, it makes that which humans have developed in the world otherworldly. This abstraction goes against the human inclination towards practical thinking, Browning argues. He establishes a new view of existing theological ideas. Instead of Practical Theology being a sub-discipline of theology, areas like historical or systematic theology fall under the umbrella of Practical Theology. The idea of there being a philosophical or theoretical theology is only 'because we have abstracted it from its practical context. We have become mentally blind to the practical activities that both precede it and follow it.'[10] Browning uses the example of several religious communities as case studies for this particular idea. He states that theology does not have to come from academics who theorize and test out their theories in practice. Instead, Practical Theology can be found in the communities that are already living out theology. The practice of theology in these communities *is* theology. As a result, Browning does not require that all theology necessarily be perfect in its practice. Inevitably, there will be interpretative issues as a result of the human aspect of theology. He states:

> [These communities], in various ways, are carriers of practical reason and exhibit many features of practical theological thinking. They do not always exhibit *good* practical theological thinking and action; that is not my claim. My claim is that they exhibit discernible features of practical theology and religiously informed practical reason – at least in some fashion and to some degree.[11]

Browning goes on to define his understanding of a fundamental Practical Theology. He describes the theological task of Christian communities as being a dialogue between Christian texts and theology in history. In the midst of this dialogue, Christian communities are also dialoguing with one another to develop theological understanding that will guide them forward.

Browning discusses the work of the German philosopher Hans-Georg Gadamer in order to further his claim about the understanding of how humans process theological knowledge. Gadamer believes that people are incapable of being completely objective in their relationship with information. He does not necessarily see this subjectiveness as being negative – instead he believes that this bias is part of the process of understanding information. He pushes back against an Enlightenment-based understanding of knowledge whereby people must be emptied of prejudice in order to obtain a pure understanding of something. Instead, Gadamer views the lens through which people view information as part of the interpretative process. A key aspect in this, however, is that people must acknowledge that these biases exist, and that their information is being filtered through this lens. The problem, according to Gadamer and Browning, is that people often view their interpretative filters as being standard and normative. As a result, an individual's bias becomes what they believe to be the absolute norm on a subject. By reflecting on these biases, people can then see the aspects of life that they are normalizing through their own lens.

The process of theological development, according to Gadamer and advocated by Browning, is through reflecting on one's practices and the meaning that is found within those practices. It is also acknowledging the bias that led to these practices being seen as 'correct' or 'true'. This reflection is what we bring back to the texts/historical theology as a means of testing. Such testing is undertaken with the knowledge that the texts/theologies have already influenced the practices that one is undertaking. This process of practice to theory and back to theory continues on a cyclical loop that results in Practical Theology. In other words, practice forms the questions that we bring back to the texts and to historical theology and, as a result, our understandings of texts and theology are influenced by these answers and so on. Or, as stated by Browning: 'It is a practical process of putting the theory-laden questions that emerge from contemporary praxis to the great religious monuments of the religious tradition.'[12]

Contemporary Practical Theology

Further defining of the field of Practical Theology has taken place in the past 20 years, both in the US context as well as in Europe (and beyond).[13] In the earlier part of this period there is further development in relation to the definitions of Practical Theology. Professor Alistair Campbell, Emeritus Director and Visiting Professor at the Centre for Biomedical Ethics at the National University of Singapore, gives three distinct reasons why this continued defining takes place. First, there is the historic belief that Practical Theology was simply applied dogmatic/systematic theology. According to Campbell, this does not serve either dogmatic theologians or Practical Theologians. On the one hand, it takes away Practical Theology's status as an independent academic discipline. On the other hand, from the point of view of Practical Theologians, it presents dogmatic theology as irrelevant because of its strictly theoretical nature. As a result, the two subjects continued to move further apart in theological thought.

Second, in terms of defining the discipline there is the Enlightenment argument concerning the place of Practical Theology within theological institutions. Is Practical Theology an art or is it a science? This is ultimately a question of academic legitimacy or even academic appropriateness. For many years, as has been discussed, Practical Theology was seen as being only for those who were in ministry. This pigeon-holing of the subject caused a sense of isolation among Practical Theologians. According to Campbell, 'Such a development meant that the discipline became divorced from the important new movements in systematic theology and biblical studies. Far from being the "crown" of divinity it became its poor relation.'[14] Third, the most unfortunate development for Practical Theology, according to Campbell, was the idea that only 'religiously-minded'[15] people were concerned with Practical Theology, thus continuing the isolation within theological institutions. Not only was Practical Theology seen as lacking scientific rigour, it was seen as being only important to a certain ministerial section of society. These three developments caused Practical Theology to fall out of favour in the academic community. Positions and Chairs in Practical Theology were in the universities of Europe in the twentieth century, but they were seen as serving a particular community and not as being a subject that was accessible to the wider academic setting. Practical Theologians took on board these three criticisms of the subject, and consequently attempted to address these criticisms through further definitions of their field.

Tackling the false dichotomy of contemplative knowledge versus practice knowledge, Duncan Forrester, Professor of Christian Ethics and Practical Theology at Edinburgh University, took on the task of offering further definitions of Practical Theology as an academic subject. Forrester challenged the historical view of the difference between *vita contemplativa* (theory) versus *vita activa* (practice), whereby ancient philosophers regarded theory as the pinnacle of human knowledge. According to Forrester, if we use this dichotomy it sets up Practical Theology as applied theology or applied theory when it is used in a given context. He stated:

> Practical Theology is not applied theology, if that term implies that the practical theologian receives ready-made the results fed in by the biblical and systematic theologians ... the practical theologians' distinctive contribution arises from a special concern with the contemporary *context*, *relevance*, and *relation* to the practice of the message preached.[16]

The importance of this definition is twofold. On the one hand, Forrester is discrediting the philosophical duality of theory and practice. Practical Theology is not applied theology, as would fit in the either/or paradigm. Additionally, Forrester offers a definition of Practical Theology as being concerned with the way that theology is practised in a given place and time, as well as how theology relates to this world in terms of importance and influence.

Gerben Heitink, Professor of Practical Theology at the Free University in the Netherlands, wrote that Practical Theology could be viewed as a 'theory of crisis'.[17] What Heitink is referencing in this context is that people turn to Practical Theology when there are changes in society that cause the Christian church to appear out of touch with the world at large. Tradition, as it operates within the church, comes under fire by society in this scenario. As a result, Practical Theologians are consulted about the way that theology should be enacted in a world that has rejected traditional ways of doing church. Heitink sees this as unique to the discipline of Practical Theology, and also believes that it serves as a strength for the subject. Because of the fluid nature of Practical Theology, there is the ability to reinterpret tradition in light of the society around the church. Accordingly, Practical Theology serves as an interpretative space that acknowledges the human nature of theology in a way that is not as prevalent in areas such as dogmatic or systematic theology. Heitink offers a definition of Practical Theology that takes this interpretation into consideration. He states: 'In this book practical theology as a theory of action is the empirically-oriented theological theory of the mediation of the Christian faith in the praxis of modern society.'[18] In this definition, Heitink points out two important areas of Practical Theology. First, the idea that Practical Theology is, at a basic level, human action of Christian beliefs. This acknowledges the undeniable human nature of theology that is so important to an understanding of Practical Theology. The other area that Heitink points out in this definition is that this human action takes place in a given society at a given time. And while the idea of context is a given in most subjects, the implication of this definition is that the contextual nature of all theology means that society has an influence on theological beliefs. In other words, that all beliefs are not necessarily God-given, but are human-constructed theories that are acted out in a certain way at a certain time and place. The empirical aspect of the definition also says that in the midst of all this action there is a possibility to observe and interpret these actions in the world using social scientific methods. The subjective nature of this definition may seem unstable to systematic or dogmatic theologians, but Heitink (and other

Practical Theologians) would argue that this is theology as we know it.

In 2000, there was one of the first attempts to create a comprehensive reader/textbook in the field of Practical Theology: *The Blackwell Reader in Pastoral and Practical Theology*[19] edited by James Woodward and Stephen Pattison. The latter was a Professor in Practical Theology at Birmingham University and James Woodward was an honorary research fellow at Cardiff University. Their book cites many of the scholars who tend to recur in Practical Theology texts, and they offer perspectives on where the field was in the year 2000. Of particular interest to my project is the chapter titled 'An Introduction to Pastoral and Practical Theology' by Woodward and Pattison. Here they attempt to systematically define Practical Theology and pastoral theology. The most important area of the definition of Practical Theology, according to the authors, is understanding that theology is fundamentally practical in nature:

> [Practical Theology] is concerned with actions, issues, and events that are of human significance in the contemporary world ... If practical theology fails to take into account the realities of the contemporary human condition, or if it produces high-flown theory that cannot be understood or applied in practice, it is arguable that it forsakes an important part of its identity and value.[20]

Alongside defining Practical Theology through this focus on the practical, Richard Osmer also focuses on the idea that Practical Theology can simultaneously see the practice of theology *as it is* and also *how it ought to be* in the contemporary world. The understanding of how theology ought to be will no doubt be different depending on one's theological perspective. This is why there is a strong emphasis on reflection and reflective practice in this type of research. However, there is a need for Practical Theologians to be able to analyse theological practices with regard to a set of standards that offers a positive effect in the contemporary world. That being said, 'Practical

Theology, however, is more interested in asking good questions about the nature of reality and practice than in trying to confine them within the restraints of traditional theological orthodoxy.'[21]

Eric Stoddart, Lecturer in Practical Theology at the University of St Andrews, continues with the theme of the human nature of Practical Theology. Referencing a quote from Stanley Hauerwas about the nature of the church, Stoddart offers a key task for Practical Theology: 'The ethical task of the Church starts not with the seemingly obvious question, "What should we do?" but "What is going on?" For Hauerwas, this involved properly appreciating the world as mad and irrational.'[22] What Stoddart (and Hauerwas) offer in this description is akin to Heitink's understanding, which has been mentioned above. There is an acknowledgement of the human element of theology. Practical Theology in this sense is not how we *should* be in the world, but what we *are* being in the world. Also, there is the recognition that the world is not without influence on the theology that people are living. The world is mad and irrational, and this designation is important as it highlights that this madness can creep into a human interpretation of theological ideas. Whether a theologian believes that theology comes from God, is God-inspired, is interpretations of sacred texts or sacred actions in the world, or is simply a human construction of God, in this definition the divine nature of theology is filtered through the earth-based human colander. What remains after the act of filtering is the essence of Practical Theology.

A group of scholars worth noting is the 'Lived Theology' project that is located at the University of Virginia. In 2017, a collection of academics came together to discuss this particular project. What is interesting about this development is that Practical Theology is all but ignored in relation to the project and the consequent text (despite many of the scholars in the Lived Theology edited collection having featured heavily in Practical Theology texts previously). In fact, Mary McClintock-Fulkerson is one of the only scholars who even mentions the obvious connection between that which is deemed Lived Theology and what is seen as Practical Theology. She offers the following: 'Theology at its most profound has always been "practical" in some sense. And since formation and lived "knowledge" of God necessarily require assessments of one's situation and the parameters of faithful response, "practical" entails conviction, reflection and much more.'[23]

The culminative text of the Lived Theology group is helpful for this book because it is so current in its viewpoints, but there is the very obvious elephant in the room in relation to its connection to the field of Practical Theology. It seems to be re-creating the wheel in terms of subject matter that has previously been covered by scholars in the field of Practical Theology. The US–UK divide in relation to Practical Theology is known, as the USA tended to maintain the pre-Browning understanding of Practical Theology as ministerial in nature. The UK and Europe continued to expand the field of Practical Theology to the secular world. As a result, the field grew in subject matter exponentially in the European context. The USA continued to see Practical Theology in the realm of the church, and as a result you had projects like the Lived Theology group who have developed Practical Theology in the secular US context. This approach is viewed as innovative, and while it certainly is in the context of the USA, it is building on work that has already been developed in other parts of the world. This is simply to note the difference in the context. As a scholar who was educated in the USA and the UK, and who has taught in both contexts as well, it is a point of aggravation. It further complicates an already complicated field that is desperately in need of clarifying itself.

In the later part of the past 20 years, one finds that Practical Theology has begun to feel more confident in its position. Gone is the continual need for definitions, but instead there is more innovation in relation to the definitions that already exist in our tradition. Accordingly, the boundaries that are so clear in other theological disciplines bend and contract because of the freedom that is inherent in the study of theology in practice. While the definitions of Practical Theology remain an area of interest for scholars, there has been a shift to the use of research methodologies as a means of defining what type of Practical Theology you are doing as opposed to endless introductions to the history of the subject. It is not as important, as a result, to have an absolute definition of Practical Theology. It is far more important to know what type of research you are doing in Practical Theology and, accordingly, what type of research methods you will use. The methods/methodology that is chosen for a project defines the project. So while some scholars continued to languish in the definitions of the field, others began to move towards finding their definitions within the context of the type of research they are doing under the banner of Practical Theology.

One way to go about this particular means of defining is to say what Practical Theology is with regard to research. Kathleen Cahalan, Professor of Theology at St John's School of Theology, and Gordon Mikoski, Associate Professor of Christian Education at Princeton Theological Seminary, have moved away from defining Practical Theology with a sentence or two and instead they focus on discussing the key features of a typical Practical Theology project. First, Practical Theology is highly attentive to how theory and practice interact in the world. Second, perhaps obviously, Practical Theology is interested in practice. It is focused on the embodiment of the theory (or theology), whether this be in rites and rituals or other means of performance related to religious practice. Another aspect that defines a Practical Theology project is that it takes seriously the holistic nature of humanity. As a result, in order to truly understand Practical Theology, a scholar must also understand the multi-faceted nature of what it means to be human. This involves physical and emotional aspects of humanity as well as the sociological aspects that make us who we are. Accordingly, in order to truly understand the human condition, scholars of Practical Theology must use interdisciplinary research methods. Specifically, theologians must have a keen sense of social scientific methods. This is vital in doing research in the practice of theology, as one must be able to understand human subjects as well as societal influences. One must also be able to know the correct means of collecting information in these realms.[24] What the information gathered means theologically is debated within Practical Theology, as Cahalan and Mikoski note:

> Practical Theologians often make the case that the meaning of traditional theological teachings cannot be known apart from testing or assessment in human life. Others argue that traditional theological tenets need revision or even fundamental reworking in the light of contemporary human experience. Some even make the bold case that new theological insight can come about through empirically based investigations of human experiences in particular contexts.[25]

The idea that theology is interpreted in the same way in every context, even 'traditional' theology, is one that Practical Theologians often challenge. Realistically, this seems to be obvious as one looks around at the variety of Christian denominations and divisions. In the context of this book, I will be looking at the ways the traditional texts have been interpreted in oppressive ways, despite many of the theological ideas being what one might consider 'traditional' or 'orthodox'. This identification of theological beliefs is another task within the context of research in Practical Theology. To name, and then to question, is the task of any Practical Theologian. According to Cahalan and Mikoski, 'Practical Theologians are unapologetic change agents.'[26]

One of the most recent books on defining Practical Theology in relation to research methods is *Invitation to Research in Practical Theology*[27] by Zoë Bennett, Elaine Graham, Stephen Pattison and Heather Walton. The authors offer further views on the importance of research in the field of Practical Theology. The rise of interest in the subject in recent years is no surprise to the authors. In the wake of what they refer to as the 'postmodern fragmentation',[28] it is increasingly difficult to speak about ideas related to theology (or any subject) in relation to absolutes. As a result, that which is considered moral or good is seen in relation to practice, not theory. They speak of the practice of theology in the ways of performance, or the way we 'perform our truths'.[29] So the way to understand theology is through these performances that take place in a variety of contexts. According to the authors, 'Christian practice is always already theological insofar as it is informed by received, performed tradition.'[30] Therefore, one question that might come out of this statement is how one defines what Christian theology is. The authors state that a certain community of tradition, such as Christianity, is 'constructed as more or less authentic'.[31] Performing your truths in a certain affirming group or in accordance with certain historical traditions means that one is attempting to fit into a particular theological community. The key bit to point out here, however, is that these norms are constructed by humans in this context. Practising your theology in a certain way will place you as an insider or an outsider of certain communities, but your orthodoxy to a tradition is only dependent on that community's understanding of the tradition. The authors use these ideas as a framework for researching theology at large, but the implications of these ideas will prove important in this book.

A scholar who very much wanted to use method/methodology as a means of defining Practical Theology is Richard Osmer. He is the Ralph B. and Helen S. Ashenfelter Professor of Mission and Evangelism at Princeton Theological Seminary. Osmer published the text *Practical Theology: An Introduction*[32] in 2008 and it represented a key marker of where the field had developed up to this point in history. Osmer offered his thoughts on the most important aspects of Practical Theology as it moved into the twenty-first century. He begins his work by discussing the core tasks of practical theological *interpretation*. Osmer is not describing how theology should be acted out, but instead is describing ways that Practical Theologians are able to study what *is* playing out before them. Osmer begins describing this framework for research by saying that there are four questions that all Practical Theologians ask when examining the practices of theology in the world:

1 What is going on?
2 Why is this going on?
3 What ought to be going on?
4 How might we respond?[33]

Osmer mentions the questions as being a guiding force within practical theological interpretations and responses; and these questions frame a practical theological methodological approach in their questioning. The questions frame the theological tasks or research methods that Osmer sees as being the key tasks of research in Practical Theology. His naming of these tasks are as follows:

1 Descriptive-empirical task
2 Interpretative task
3 Normative task
4 Pragmatic task.[34]

The descriptive-empirical task refers to the method of observing contexts, situations or groups and describing what is taking place with regard to generalizations that might be inferred. The interpretative task looks to attempt to explain why these particular generalizations about a context, situation or group might be occurring. This method of interpretation draws heavily on the areas of social scientific analysis to come to conclusions that highlight the 'Why?' of a situation. The normative task looks to respond to what is happening in a given context, situation or group in order to evaluate (based on ethical norms or theological developments) whether 'good practice'[35] is occurring. Finally, the pragmatic method is akin to the conclusion of action research as a method. It looks to engage with a context, situation or community after they have been looked at in reference to the normative task. The response from the community, and indeed the dialogue that occurs as a result of such a normative task, is the pragmatic conclusion to Practical Theology as research.[36]

I will be using Osmer's Practical Theology methodology as the framework for my analysis of the examples in Part II of this book. The descriptive task in each example will offer information on the Practical Theology of a situation. The interpretative task will look at how this theological conclusion (or interpretation) came to be. The focus in each chapter will be the normative task, which looks to see the ways that each example represents oppressive Practical Theology. Finally, there will be conclusions that examine in what ways these theological conclusions still haunt society. Discussing what should be done in relation to bad theology is interesting, as these cases are largely historical (though their implications remain). What to do then becomes more of a project on how to spot these theological conclusions when they happen, and also how not to repeat these unique examples of bad theology.

The Wiley-Blackwell Companion to Practical Theology

It would be remiss of me, in my conclusions on the current definitions of Practical Theology, to leave out the latest textbook on the topic. The most recent summary of the state of Practical Theology in a comprehensive book is *The Wiley-Blackwell Companion to Practical Theology*.[37] This text attempts to bring together a collection of scholars who can offer insights into where we are as Practical Theologians, as well as showing where we may need to go in the future.

The significance of *The Wiley-Blackwell Companion* for the field of Practical Theology cannot be overstated. Since the nineteenth century, Practical Theology has grown and evolved in different time periods and contexts. The *Companion* attempted to place a flag in the sand and offer an overview of where the field resides in the current era of academia. The editor of the *Companion* is Bonnie Miller-McLemore, who is E. Rhodes and Leona B. Carpenter Professor of Pastoral Theology at Vanderbilt University Divinity School and Graduate Department of Religion. A well-known scholar of Practical Theology, Miller-McLemore assembled together a group of scholars who wrote chapters on a variety of different areas within the field of Practical Theology.

The text itself is divided into four parts. The first part discusses Practical Theology as a way of life. In other words, it offers a variety of ways in which the practice of theology occurs in our day-to-day lives, outside the confines of the theological institution or the church. The second part looks at method, and the means by which scholars of Practical Theology conduct quantitative and qualitative research. The third part is a mixed one that offers sections related to ministerial education as well as academic theological education. This includes areas like Pastoral Care, Worship and Spirituality as well as Systematic Theology and Contextual Education. The fourth part looks at Practical Theology in a variety of specific contexts. First, it is discussed in relation to the 'isms' – areas like racism, sexism, classism and so on. This part continues by addressing global incarnations of Practical Theology in a variety of countries throughout the world. It ends with a look into Practical Theology in four particular traditions: mainline Protestantism, Roman Catholicism, Protestant Evangelicalism and Pentecostalism.

The *Companion* has been praised for being an important marker as to where the field of Practical Theology stands in this current time period. It offers a good spread of topics, and it shows how many subjects fall under the umbrella of this academic field. It also includes many of the more prominent scholars in relation to Practical Theology. The *Companion* shows not only the different subjects that Practical Theology encompasses, but also the different ways in which it can be understood. From theology in life, to theological methods, to theological education and even theology in geographic areas and traditions, the *Companion* shows how scholars have continued to develop Practical Theology in a multitude of directions. Finally, and most practically for educators, it serves as a textbook that can easily be used in a teaching setting.

The Wiley-Blackwell Companion to Practical Theology, though, has not been without its critics, including myself. In 2014, Eric Stoddart offered a chapter in his book *Advancing Practical Theology* titled 'Case Study: *The Wiley-Blackwell Companion to Practical Theology* – The Neoliberal, Imperialist Elephant in the Room?'[38] Stoddart points out the importance of the text as a contribution to the field of Practical Theology, but also sees areas where the text itself could be improved. His emphasis is on a lack of liberation-orientated frameworks within the context of the chapters, along with the US-centric nature of the scholars who were chosen for the selections within the text. Collectively, it means that there can be a very parochial view of Practical Theology, according to Stoddart. There is also a lack of self-criticism in relation to the scholars who are from the USA and from the current political situation (as it stood at the time of publication). Stoddart states: 'Reading the 600 pages you would never know that Practical Theology is a discipline performed in a world with multiple wars and a vast military complex of US superiority.'[39] Accordingly, many of the chapters are tinted with the middle-class US situation as opposed to engaging actively with minority or oppressed groups. Stoddart notices, as do I, that there is little engagement with US politics from these US authors. He states: 'There is something of a blind spot here, because in the chapter on the Protestant evangelical context for Practical Theology there is but a small mention of the Religious Right – but it is historical.'[40] Ultimately, Stoddart is concerned that the book does not acknowledge the power struggles throughout the world, despite the US Practical Theologians who ·are writing. He observes that this might be a result of marketing the book in the USA, but also notes that the lack of topics related to areas of liberation and self-reflection are an obvious failing in the publication.

The importance of Stoddart's critique of the *Companion* lies not only in the fact that I share many of his views, but also because my reading of both texts inspired my book. My sense when I was reading the *Companion* was that Practical Theology was being made to seem very American and very OK. The struggles that Practical Theology has gone through over the years to legitimize itself could have been further elaborated. Stoddart's point about the lack of self-reflection of the US academics is also very clear in the text. There are many opportunities in the *Companion* to talk about the response of Practical Theology to issues related to war, oppression and indeed liberation. These issues are largely omitted. The text reads as a great summary of certain aspects of Practical Theology, but it ultimately feels very *nice*. And by 'nice' I would even go so far as to say salvific. In other words, Practical Theology is portrayed as a means to help some of these tragic 'isms', but there is little discussion as to how it might have led to some of the very 'isms' it is fighting against.

My readings of the *Companion* led me to contemplate the future of Practical Theology. The *Companion* might be a consumable summary of friends of Practical Theology (and their specialties), but does it reflect where Practical Theology is going in the future, or even realistically where it sits at the moment? My own work in constructing theological views of both violence and peacebuilding in war-torn countries would suggest that this is not the case. The shocking omission that I found in the *Companion* (and other texts of Practical Theology) is the assumption that the practice of theology is uncritically positive; in other words, that Practical Theology is a corrective on the ills that infect our world in a million different ways. Humans construct theology, and as a result this theology is not always as 'nice' as that portrayed in the *Companion*. We do ourselves a great disservice in the field of Practical Theology if we are not able to see this omission.

The future of Practical Theology

Many theologians have written texts contemplating the future of Practical Theology at various points in history. A most recent addition to this collection is *Opening the Field of Practical Theology: An Introduction*,[41] edited by Kathleen A. Cahalan and Gordon S. Mikoski. In this text, the editors gather together a diverse group of scholars who are looking, as the title suggests, to open up the field of Practical Theology to under-represented groups. This aligns with the hopes of Eric Stoddart in his text about advancing Practical Theology. Although there is an uncomfortable relationship between liberation theology and Practical Theology, there is enough of an overlap in method and theory such that the two subjects can dialogue with each other in the context of theological studies.

In one chapter of *Opening the Field*, Katherine Turpin discusses this uncomfortable relationship between liberation theology and Practical Theology. It is titled, aptly, 'Liberationist Practical Theology'. In this chapter, Turpin addresses the glaring fact that Practical Theologians tend not to engage with their liberation theology colleagues. She acknowledges the dangers in combining subjects into a consumable package, but she also thinks there are benefits to engagement between the two subjects. She writes:

> While I want to avoid affixing a label to liberation theologians that many of them would not claim for themselves, the similarities between liberation theology and practical theology in terms of contextual grounding and analysis, dialogue between human experience and normative strands of the Christian tradition, and proposals for renewed and transformed practice are striking.[42]

In many ways this dialogue feels like an important development in the future of Practical Theology. Like other theological subjects, Practical Theology fell into the pattern of highlighting only the viewpoints of those scholars who fit into certain acceptable paradigms within the study of theology. *Opening the Field* addresses this by including chapters on less-represented voices within the context of Practical Theology. It also has a chapter titled 'White Practical Theology', by Tom Beaudoin and Katherine Turpin, which acknowledges that all theology is constructed in a time and place, even theology that is viewed as dogmatic or orthodox. This chapter pays attention to the fact that, like many of the 'contextual' theologies throughout the world, there is a theology that is closely related to white/European/North American theologians. This theological position has its own assumptions and outcomes and is not something that should be seen as a categorical norm within the context of theological studies (as it has been previously). According to the authors of the chapter:

> In Christian Theology, the history of a variety of white movements, from the more positive nineteenth century abolitionist movements to the more abhorrent Christian identity movements have expressed this cultural norm of belief in progress. Many white people are historically incentivized to believe they can co-create with God to build a better world ...[43]

The authors, importantly, highlight here the very whiteness in the field of Practical Theology. They also point out the ways that Practical Theology has been constructed to be incredibly positive and also abhorrent. This is an important distinction, because it shows that the authors recognize that the theology created in these contexts can produce both positive and negative results; and that in both cases they can be viewed as normative because of the standing of those who are producing the theology – which in this case is white theologians.

Similarly to Stoddart, the authors of this text criticize the *Companion* for its assumptions in relation to Practical Theology. The contributors are quick to offer observations of the background of some of the authors who are writing the framing chapters for the *Companion*: 'All of these framing chapters are themselves white, and class-based determinations are evident throughout, with references to vacations and conspicuous consumption.'[44] The authors writing in *Opening the Field* (one of whom is included in the *Companion*) are not trying to excuse how Practical Theology has operated under an umbrella of white theological contributions, but instead they are looking to the future of the field to do a better job of including alternative voices. The chapter 'White Practical Theology' was not in the original version of the book, because theologians have long acknowledged this historical bias. However, the contributors to the volume pushed for it to be included. This is an important inclusion, because it shows how Practical Theology has traditionally operated in an echo chamber of similar voices. It is a humbling observation, and it shows that Practical Theologians are able to hold up a mirror to their own biases and discrimination.

Another key development in the future of Practical Theology relates to a need to move towards a liberationist Practical Theology. This development is in relation to the authorship of theology as a whole. 'Contextual Theology as Practical Theology', by Stephen Bevans, helps the reader to see the examination of theology as human construct as being one of the principal tasks of Practical Theology. Bevans begins his chapter with the sentence: 'All theology is contextual theology.'[45] Bevans came to this conclusion while studying theology in Europe. He began to realize that the theology that he was learning was influenced heavily by the context in which it developed (European-based in Roman/Greek thought). Consequently, he observed that the majority of those who adhered to the Christian tradition (for example, those in the southern hemisphere) were not being represented by the theology that was being produced in Europe. The understanding of 'contextual' theology can be contentious, and my students are well aware of my dislike of the term. The idea behind contextual, however, is of the utmost importance. The acknowledgement that all theology has a context is fundamental to theological education. That being said, my firm belief is that when one lumps all theologies that are not white/Western/European/

traditional into one category of 'contextual', scholars are re-creating the problem they hoped to fix.

The importance of acknowledging the contextual nature of all theology is not just in the liberative vein of inclusivity of voices. It is also to highlight that theology that was seen as being without context, or traditional, or orthodox, was instead very contextual. Bevans offers the following examples of why this movement took hold globally, writing that there was:

> a general dissatisfaction in many places and among many peoples with traditional, Western approaches to theology; a growing awareness that such approaches are not just irrelevant but oppressive; the rise of nationalism after the demise of colonialization; the renaissance of local religions; and the relatively recent 'empirical' notion of culture over and against 'classicist' understandings.[46]

The importance of the context of theology, as well as the practice of theology within that context, is not lost on Bevans, and he ties it directly to Practical Theology: 'Every practical theology is a contextual theology, but not every contextual theology is a practical theology.'[47] Bevans goes on to explain how the two fields of study are connected. Both Practical Theology and contextual theology see the context (of that within which something is being practised) as being hugely important to the ultimate theological conclusions that are made by a person or a community. So, in turn, both the practice of theology and the community (context) where one is practising theology are deeply influential on theology as a whole. Bevans argues that 'Contextual theologians understand that theology involves not so much content (although it certainly has content) as process. The aim of theology is not to work out a system that is enduring so much as to meet everyday experiences with faith.'[48] Bevans claims that part of the task of Practical Theology is that of describing humanity's constructions of theological truths in context. These theological truths are most likely to be observed in practice, where they are seen in their performative form.

They will be contextual in nature, as they will be worked by individuals in a certain time and place.

Accordingly, a key task for the future of Practical Theology is noting that there is a lack of liberative voices in many of our texts while recognising that this lack is a result of the nature of Practical Theology (white/European/American constructions of theology). Alongside noting our most 'popular' texts as constructions of theological insights, Practical Theologians in the future may want to engage with 'non-popular' texts to see in what ways our popular constructions may or may not limit alternative voices from coming through in the discipline. So while we construct, and as we describe that which is constructed, we also reflect. In these reflections we hope to find the oppressive twists or the liberative turns that may lead to change. It is with this idea of construction in mind that we move to the next chapter.

Notes

1 Mary McClintock Fulkerson, 'Ethnography in Theology' in *Lived Theology*, ed. Charles Marsh, Peter Slade and Sarah Azaransky (Oxford: Oxford University Press, 2017), p. 127.

2 Eric Stoddart, *Advancing Practical Theology: Critical Discipleship for Disturbing Times* (London: SCM Press, 2014), p. 19.

3 Terrance Tice, 'Editor's Postscript' in Friedrich Schleiermacher, *Brief Outline of Theology as a Field of Study*, 3rd edn, trans. Terrance Tice (Louisville, KY: Westminster John Knox Press, 2011), p. 137.

4 Tice, 'Editor's Postscript', p. 129.

5 Schleiermacher, *Brief Outline of Theology*, p. 43.

6 Schleiermacher, *Brief Outline of Theology*, p. 30.

7 In my own work I discuss this idea of the hierarchy of theological disciplines (see Leah E. Robinson, 'Practical Theology in Scotland: Embracing Disinheritance', *Practical Theology* 10.3 (2017), pp. 221–35). I argue that Practical Theology has been seen as a lesser theological discipline as a result of three developments: theology being baptized as exact knowledge of God; Practical Theology using social scientific methods; and Practical Theology being typecast as only involving the church.

8 Don Browning, *A Fundamental Practical Theology* (Minneapolis, MN: Fortress Press, 1995), p. 3.

9 Browning, *A Fundamental Practical Theology*, p. 5.

10 Browning, *A Fundamental Practical Theology*, pp. 8–9.

11 Browning, *A Fundamental Practical Theology*, p. 12 (my italics).

12 Browning, *A Fundamental Practical Theology*, p. 139.

13 While there are many Practical Theologians who could be discussed in these sections, I have chosen ones who fit with the project at hand, keeping in mind that there is far more literature on the subject to explore.

14 Alistair Campbell, 'The Nature of Practical Theology' in *Theology and Practice*, ed. Duncan B. Forrester (London: Epworth Press, 1990), p. 11.

15 Campbell, 'The Nature of Practical Theology', p. 12.

16 Duncan B. Forrester, 'Divinity in Use and Practice' in *Theology and Practice*, ed. Duncan B. Forrester (London: Epworth Press, 1990), pp. 7–8 (my italics).

17 G. Rau quoted in Gerben Heitink, *Practical Theology* (Grand Rapids, MI: William B. Eerdmans, 1993), p. 3.

18 Heitink, *Practical Theology*, p. 6.

19 James Woodward and Stephen Pattison, eds, *The Blackwell Reader in Pastoral and Practical Theology* (Oxford: Blackwell Publishing, 2000).

20 James Woodward and Stephen Pattison, 'An Introduction to Pastoral and Practical Theology' in *The Blackwell Reader in Pastoral and Practical Theology* (Oxford: Blackwell Publishing, 2000), p. 7.

21 Woodward and Pattison, 'Introduction to Pastoral and Practical Theology', p. 15.

22 Stoddart, *Advancing Practical Theology*, p. 15.

23 Mary McClintock-Fulkerson, 'Ethnography in Theology' in *Lived Theology*, ed. Charles Marsh, Peter Slade and Sarah Azaransky (Oxford: Oxford University, 2017), p. 117.

24 Kathleen A. Cahalan and Gordon S. Mikoski, eds, *Opening the Field of Practical Theology* (Lanham, MD: Rowman & Littlefield, 2014), pp. 2–5.

25 Cahalan and Mikoski, *Opening the Field of Practical Theology*, p. 5.

26 Cahalan and Mikoski, *Opening the Field of Practical Theology*, p. 6.

27 Zoë Bennett, Elaine Graham, Stephen Pattison and Heather Walton, *Invitation to Research in Practical Theology* (Abingdon: Routledge, 2018).

28 Bennett, Graham, Pattison and Walton, *Invitation to Research in Practical Theology*, p. 72.

29 Bennett, Graham, Pattison and Walton, *Invitation to Research in Practical Theology*, p. 72.

30 Bennett, Graham, Pattison and Walton, *Invitation to Research in Practical Theology*, p. 72.

31 Bennett, Graham, Pattison and Walton, *Invitation to Research in Practical Theology*, pp. 72–3.

32 Richard Osmer, *Practical Theology: An Introduction* (Grand Rapids, MI: William B. Eerdmans, 2008).

33 Osmer, *Practical Theology: An Introduction*, p. 4.

34 This is a similar framework to Heitink's *Practical Theology*. Osmer, *Practical Theology: An Introduction*, p. 4.

35 Osmer, *Practical Theology: An Introduction*, p. 4.

36 Osmer, *Practical Theology: An Introduction*, p. 4.

37 Bonnie Miller-McLemore, ed., *The Wiley-Blackwell Companion to Practical Theology* (Oxford: Wiley-Blackwell Publishing, 2014).

38 Stoddart, *Advancing Practical Theology*, p. 108.

39 Stoddart, *Advancing Practical Theology*, pp. 116–17.

40 Stoddart, Advancing Practical Theology, p. 117.

41 Cahalan and Mikoski, *Opening the Field of Practical Theology*.

42 Katherine Turpin, 'Liberationist Practical Theology' in *Opening the Field of Practical Theology*, ed. Kathleen A. Cahalan and Gordon S. Mikoski (Lanham, MD: Rowman & Littlefield, 2014), p. 156.

43 Tom Beaudoin and Katherine Turpin, 'White Practical Theology', in *Opening the Field of Practical Theology*, ed. Kathleen A. Cahalan and Gordon S. Mikoski (Lanham, MD: Rowman & Littlefield, 2014), p. 256.

44 Beaudoin and Turpin, 'White Practical Theology', p. 263.

45 Stephen Bevans, 'Contextual Theology as Practical Theology' in *Opening the Field of Practical Theology*, ed. Kathleen A. Cahalan and Gordon S. Mikoski (Lanham, MD: Rowman & Littlefield, 2014), p. 45.

46 Bevans, 'Contextual Theology as Practical Theology', p. 47.

47 Bevans, 'Contextual Theology as Practical Theology', p. 54.

48 Bevans, 'Contextual Theology as Practical Theology', p. 49.

2

The Methodology:
Creating God in our Image

Constructing theology as a key task of Practical Theology

Faced with an incredibly disparate and complex set of
materials, the theologian is always ultimately making meaning rather than finding it. No fixed rules or established cultural patterns predetermine proper theological construction
or relieve the theologian for the decisions he/she reaches.[1]

The understanding that theology is not a unified whole,
untouched by history, is an idea that Practical Theology holds
dear. The very understanding of Practical Theology as something that can be studied via qualitative research methods,
as well as reflective practice,[2] illustrates the understanding of
theology as an observation, a dialogue, and a construction that
happens between God and humanity in the course of human
history.

Practical Theologians have differing ideas about this construction. Some see Practical Theology as applied theology.
This type of theology is known for taking the themes in historical and systematic theology and applying them to everyday
life. The results of this application can offer insights into the
way that theology is lived in the world. Other theologians see
Practical Theology as a dialogue between theological ideas and
lived context. In this scenario, the theology is lived out in the
world and, as a result, there is an influence on the theological

ideas themselves. It is a circular process of theological construction that is advocated by many contemporary Practical Theologians.[3]

What is discussed less by Practical Theologians is the idea that theology is constructed by humanity as an act of doing Practical Theology. The practical nature of taking historical doctrines (recognizing their historical construction) and applying them to a particular context is the embodiment of theology itself. Systematic and historical theology has its place, but Practical Theology asks what happens when these ideas are released into the world. The process of this embodiment involves interpretation on the part of the person who is enacting the theology. While theology itself is a human endeavour, the action of the theology is even more a human product.

As tends to happen in theology, the idea of the construction of theology as a human endeavour in itself became a theological area of study. As Jason Wyman Jr states, theology 'had found a comfortable place as a "systematic" endeavor. Responding to the rigors of the academy, historic philosophies, and the Enlightenment and modernity.'[4] According to Wyman, theology post-Enlightenment looked like a series of attempts at organizing the doctrines of the church into logical systems. And these attempts were viewed as the legitimate process by which theology was not constructed, but instead systematized.

The issue with this logic-based means of organizing theology is what happened when it became embodied. This embodiment led to a loss of a system, of logic, or even generalization. Many systematic theologians, and even more dogmatic theologians, felt as though there was an objective revelation that could be captured and codified into manuscripts. One of the clearest proponents of this method of theological understanding was Karl Barth. According to Wyman:

> For Barth, the veracity of theological claims is grounded upon divine revelation; the task of dogmatics as a critical testing and theological investigation illuminates for theologians how faithfully their theologizing has been to the

actual structure of Christianity and the grace of God. There is a fundamental assumption that a stable Christian message exists, which theologians have a responsibility to bring to light no matter how (infinitely) futile their attempts to do so are.[5]

While this perspective on theological enquiry was satisfying (especially to the church), it seemed to many in a post-Enlightenment world to be incredibly assumptive. Questions relating to the who, what and where with regard to authority in theology began to emerge among scholars who felt that much of the theological material that was produced by both dogmatics and systematic theologians was not representative of the lived practice of theology.

While stopping short of dismissing the systemization of church doctrines, the theologian Paul Tillich challenged the idea of theology as a science that was capable of remaining unchanged in a changing world. Tillich states: 'In every assumedly scientific theology there is a point where individual experience, traditional valuation, and personal commitment must decide the issue.'[6] One might infer from this statement that a system of theology was only systematic in so much as it was not applied, as long as it wasn't practically being lived. Once that theology was embodied, the systematic nature of the theology was lost in the midst of human action.

Consequent theologians seized upon this idea. For many, the idea of theology as an ahistorical, universal set of dogmas or systematized theological ideas that represented one clear truth for all people was not tenable. As early as the 1900s, theologians began using the term 'constructive' in relation to theology. In 1907, Herbert Alden Youtz wrote about constructive theology as an alternative to systematic or dogmatic theology:

Current essays in theology may be roughly classified in two groups: those which are seeking for an 'essence,' or a 'finality,' or an 'ultimate principle of unity' which expresses an unresolvable quantum in all religion, or 'essential religion' seen in its lowest terms; second, those which take current religious doctrines and try to translate them into the terms of the thought-life of today.[7]

Youtz was one of several theologians who began to question the practicality of trying to find one Christian truth in theology. It was through this development that theologians began to adopt the idea of theology as being a product of human construction. The idea of 'constructive theology' as a field of study began to take shape, most notably in the innovations of the USA-based Workgroup on Constructive Theology. Through this group a definition of constructive theology began to emerge. Wyman adopts ideas from Youtz when he offers a definition of the discipline, saying that constructive theology 'is a method of doing Christian theology that takes seriously theological and church tradition as well as modern critiques of that tradition being something universal, eternal or essential'.[8]

An important aspect of constructive theology, according to Wyman, is not the total abandonment of tradition, theologically or otherwise. The claims of those who are doing constructive theology is that the use of systematic theology is vital to what they are doing. The difference lies in the claims made by constructive theology, which admittedly remain vague. According to Wyman, though, the guiding principle of constructive theology is to not get stuck in one theological abyss that appears to be a universal truth, but instead to see that 'constructive theology is a new attitude about what *good theology is, what it does, and whom it serves*'.[9] This idea of good theology will come back into the discussion as we continue to identify theology that can be constructed in a way that is not necessarily 'good'. The development of constructive theology is a key area for this book. As a result, I will now dive into the works of two theologians who have wrestled with ideas of construction: Gordon Kaufman and Kathryn Tanner.

The Theological Imagination

> Theology is human work. Theology is done by humans for human purposes; theological work must be assessed by human standards, and its judges are themselves always ordinary human beings.[10]

Gordon Kaufman was a theologian vital to the theological framing of my book, and his understanding of the construction of theology has inspired the work of many in this particular field. Kaufman served as the Mallinckrodt Professor of Divinity at Harvard Divinity School. The text that I have chosen best fits with the theoretical viewpoint with which I will analyse theology here. As a result, it is important to understand the key concepts presented in his 1981 work, *The Theological Imagination*.

Kaufman begins this work by establishing a fundamental tenet: ideas about God are ultimately human constructs. He quickly explains the idea of God and the idea of 'reality God'[11] as being two very different concepts in theology: 'God is not a reality immediately available in our experience for observation, inspection, and description, and speech about or to God therefore is never directly referential.'[12] As a result, there is no way of truly understanding the reality God, and we need to acknowledge that we are constructing and reconstructing an understanding of God in our own context. And not only in our own context, but arguably in our image, Kaufman suggests. His view is that all notions of God are created within a particular cultural and linguistic context that is based on previous generations' developments of God.[13] Kaufman is clear that Christians have been making subjective theological decisions about the tradition from the very beginning. As an example, he argues that the construction of the Christian Bible (the text from which we gain knowledge about God) was itself a theological decision at a particular time and place.

Not only is the idea of an evolving view of God a natural product of human imagination, but Kaufman argues that this construction is vital to the continued reliance on God by humanity. People are incapable of completely understanding a concept that is outside their own lived reality, and as a result we interpret God through the lens of our 'context within which we are living and moving'. Accordingly, we are interpreters who live in a given time period and have a 'place and a role within that context'.[14] People use the building blocks of the context in which they live to construct a concept of God. God's reality is less important in this scenario, as the meaning of God to a person or community in a given context is what gives meaning to the constructed God. This lack of *direct* divine revelation from the reality God may seem problematic to some theologians, but Kaufman argues that it explains why our concept of God has been so fluid throughout the biblical texts as well as throughout history.

One's own belief in God as divinely revealing Godself to humanity remains a valid view in this framework, but there has to be an understanding that reality God can never be framed in human terms. Kaufman believes that God must be independent of humanity with regard to identification as otherwise God is no longer transcendent. To transcend means that there must be finite being(s) who set the standard of that which is knowable. According to Kaufman: 'God is thus conceived to be radically independent of all human striving and desiring certainly no product of our fantasies and wishes.'[15] Kaufman goes on to explain how people have thus constructed God in the way that they would hope God to be. A God who was worthy of devotion and sacrifice. A God who also was anthropomorphic in an emotional sense. Hence, God came to be understood as a loving God. A God who was looking out for people who God had created. According to Kaufman, God had to give humans an 'orientation of life'. God answered the questions that plagued human existence, offered people comfort in their earthly struggles and also served as a compass to guide humanity where it needed to go, both in this life and the next (salvation).

God as being a relative figure in human history is addressed by Kaufman. While the idea of God being relative (that is, based on human construction) might seem problematic for some, Kaufman offers the explanation of this relativity as being based on the finite nature of the human condition. This type of relative position offers the idea that people can never truly know about God, and this is because God is not of the same substance as humans. God is infinite. As a result, there is a distinction to be made between the truth that people are capable of creating, and that which exists in God. Theology as seen in this relative position is most obviously a human construct, in so far as true knowledge of an infinite entity is not within the grasp of a finite being. As a result, people construct the nature of God according to the context in which they live and know, and the success of this type of construction varies greatly depending on a particular person's motivations and contexts. The relative position argues that as a result of this type of human construction of God's truth (or theology, as it were), there can never be a universally accurate God knowledge.[16] Historically, theologians have called this type of theology 'contextual theology'. This term has been used to describe any theology that falls outside of the Western, white, male paradigm. As a result, it was seen by some as being less valuable in theological thinking than theology that was deemed to be 'true' and 'absolute'. Relativists push back against this idea with an understanding of the construction of theology as a natural human development throughout history.

Kaufman also offers an alternative viewpoint to relativism, which he argues can be equally problematic. This position is an absolutist one that sees the human mind as fully capable of understanding the truth of God. Absolutists reject the idea of the relativist: that the finite nature of humans means that they cannot understand God. Absolutists believe there is a universal or dogmatic truth that can be established through this connection to God. According to the absolutists, God's infinite nature means that God can offer truth to finite beings. Absolutists will inevitably criticize relativists for their view of theology as being a human construct only. This causes, according to absolutists, the idea that theology has an 'inconsistency and incoherence'[17] that is unimaginable in such an important category as God-talk. Kaufman sees this position as being a direct result of Enlightenment thinking, whereby theology had to find its place among the push towards scientific investigations. Theology became the Queen of the Sciences during this period because theologians claimed that their conclusions about God served as the ultimate truth about the world. As a result, all other claims to truth are just that – claims – until they are criticized in accordance with the theology rubric. According to Kaufman, theology was 'the last court of appeal for human understanding'.[18] These claims of absolute knowledge were based on the figure of Jesus, the text of the Bible and the traditions of the church, and as a result this perspective held the ultimate authority even in the context of a new era of developments.

Kaufman ultimately adopts a middle position between the relativists and the absolutists in his understanding of theology. That being said, he does ultimately lean towards the relativists, and puts forward the claim that people are interpreting God through a finite lens via finite understandings. He does not think, however, that the human nature of this construction means that theology is any less important as a means of understanding God. Kaufman states that although theology is a human construct, it must be self-critical as to what it is actually saying. The idea of having an absolute knowledge of God is, according to Kaufman, 'idolatry'.[19] Kaufman instead sees theology as being more of a dialogical discipline than a marker of absolute truth. Every claim that is made on behalf of theology must ultimately be criticized in relation to the claim itself, as well as the experiences of the finite person who is making the claim. Kaufman calls this dialogical building of theological learning 'Imaginative Construction'.[20] He understands that this process can be criticized by both sides of the theology argument, but he sees that human construction can be valuable in the pursuit of knowledge about God. He also sees the problems with this viewpoint, and as a result he believes that theology should be viewed with a critical lens in order to keep it honest to its finite roots. The imaginative constructive nature of theology is what keeps it relevant to the contemporary world, according to Kaufman. The idea of passing off finite ideas as absolute truth will not keep theology relevant. Kaufman wants to ensure that theology that people construct is constantly in dialogue with the world in which it exists. This is theology, according to Kaufman, and it does not have to have infallible answers in order to be important to the Christian community.

Theories of Culture

Another theologian who has discussed ideas related to the construction of theology is Kathryn Tanner at Yale University. Tanner is Frederick Marquand Professor of Systematic Theology at Yale University Divinity School. In 1997, she wrote *Theories of Culture*,[21] which looked at the connection between areas of theology and culture. For the purpose of this project, I will be focusing on Part II of Tanner's book.

In Part II, Tanner engages in the idea that culture directly influences theological developments. Not only is there an influence on theology from the culture, but she puts forth the idea that theology should be seen as being a part of culture itself. She offers the understanding that theology is a human creation. As a result, theology is limited in its scope in relation to a certain author, time period and geography (among other things). She writes: 'Theology is something human beings produce. Like all human activities, it is historically and socially conditioned; it cannot be understood in isolation from the rest of human sociocultural practices.'[22] Theology as a human endeavour is vital to the understanding of constructive theology, and also that of Practical Theology.

Tanner goes on to discuss the idea that it is not differing philosophies that cause debates within theology, as has been historically the case, but instead it is differing cultures that are in competition with one another with regard to displaying their respective authorities.[23] Tanner goes on to say that 'Anthropology insists that culture only comes in specific shapes; there is no culture in general.'[24] This is an important point, as it highlights the understanding that theology is less about one universal truth, and more about a dominant culture's truth. Accordingly, theology looks very different depending on the culture from which it comes. And while these cultural differences mean that theology can look like a beautiful patchwork quilt, it also means that theological authority can be given to a variety of different cultures at the same time. While this authority might not be viewed as legitimate by an entire religion, it can be seen as legitimate by the culture that it represents. Discussing the idea of how academic theology justifies its own practices as legitimate, Tanner further highlights how groups of cultures can self-justify their own beliefs and practices. She states:

> Theology projects onto the object studies what its own procedures of investigation requires – a coherent whole. The method of study itself thereby validates the conclusions of the theologian while disqualifying the people and practices it studies from posing a challenge to those conclusions.[25]

While in this discussion Tanner is referring to how theology is constructed in a sense that looks to 'figure out theology's connection to God's influence on human life', it can be argued that this method of constructing theology could be used as a means of cultural affirmation as opposed to being a representation of God's influence. Tanner discusses the idea that there must be some level of accountability with regard to theology. She suggests that there has to be reflection on areas of Christianity that seem to 'conflict'[26] and that there may be a need for theologians to engage in 'theological investigation'[27] when it comes to reconciling certain aspects of Christian practice with one's own Christian beliefs.

With that being said, Tanner also talks about the seemingly impossible task of defining in an objective way what it actually means to be a Christian. In order to further this discussion, she considers the idea of theologians identifying Christianity via boundaries of Christian practices as well as that of comparison and correlation with other religious traditions. Tanner agrees with aspects of previous theological conclusions in relation to Christian identity, but ultimately she sees Christian identity as a task. The task, specifically, is the continuous evaluation of what it means to have a Christian identity. This type of self-critical and self-reflecting task mean that a community is in a continuous state of evaluating what it means to be that community, otherwise known as 'a community of argument'.[28] According to Tanner, 'What it really means to be a Christian cannot be summed up in any neat formula that would allow one to know already what Christian discipleship *will prove to include or exclude* over the course of time.'[29]

Tanner concludes her book with two fundamental questions in relation to Christian identity: 'What kind of practices are Christian ones?'[30] and 'To what degree do they seek consensus or view diversity as a good?'[31] She suggests a standard understanding of what it means to be Christian (in as much as it can be established).[32] While admitting that reaching a consensus in a Christian community might be unattainable, Tanner does suggest that it might be possible to recognize the 'other' Christian community as striving for the same values and beliefs as one's own.

Within Christian communities there should be space for people to offer disagreements in relation to certain held beliefs; these disagreements should not, however, lead to chaos, according to Tanner.[33] As a result, there should be some attempts to limit the number of disagreements that take place within a community while at the same time offering space for these disagreements to occur. The community, however, should carefully observe this limiting of disagreements because of the threat of authoritarian views ruling. Instead, views should be evaluated in relation to previous Christian views held by the community, as well as how one's views relate to the 'alteration it makes to the cultural material it borrows in a particular time and place'.[34] These challenges should be made from within the community, according to Tanner. Through these challenges, the hope is that the mistakes that could potentially be made with regard to religious practice might be corrected from within. This is a valuable process, in Tanner's view, because 'human judgement is fallible'[35] and the process of evaluating claims can be a productive one for a community. Consensus might not be reached during this process, but dialogue is a far better process of construction than a monologue, and it helps to keep the Christian community together as a unit.

Practical Theology as human construction

Constructive theology actively bucks the trend of theology being put into a definitive box. This, in many ways, highlights why it has not previously been strongly associated with the field of Practical Theology. Practical Theology has worked in the opposite direction to constructive theology, as it is perpetually trying to define itself in relation to other theological disciplines.

That being said, the understanding of Practical Theology as both an action of human construction as well as the product of human construction is no new thought in our field. Accordingly, while I have spoken of other theoretical frameworks of theology, this project is first and foremost an exploration into Practical Theology. While it could be claimed that I am adopting constructive theology and calling it Practical Theology for my own purposes, those within constructive theology see this category as a methodology as opposed to a theological category. Wyman, for example, says:

Constructive theology in the end doesn't have a specific content. It, above all else, has become a methodology based in a specific attitude or 'mood' about what purpose theology serves in the world ... the only initial basis for establishing who is or isn't a constructive theologian, or what is or isn't constructive theology, will be self-naming.[36]

The fluid nature of constructive theology means that it is able to have a productive dialogue with the likes of Practical Theology. The goal of this chapter is simply to connect the two worlds to show that they are (much like lived theology and Practical Theology) doing very similar things. In many ways, constructive theology offers a more open way of understanding theology than Practical Theology. So the logical next step might be framing this work within the context of constructive theology as opposed to Practical Theology. This point is taken, but the idea of Practical Theology as both a construction and the means by which to analyse constructions in very specific, lived contexts is of the utmost importance. The very essence of Practical Theology is the action of theology in the world. The construction of said theology in the world is something that is discussed less than the actual action itself. My proposition is that the action of construction is, in itself, a practical theological activity. The constructed theology, then, is acted out in the world via the practice of theology. So constructed theology is Practical Theology in a twofold way.

Much like Practical Theology, constructive theology does not claim to be a recent development that is not historical prior to the twentieth century or the Enlightenment or Vatican II (or fill in whichever historical event where these 'contextual' theological developments are said to have just appeared). Constructive theology sees itself as being historical in nature. All of the doctrines and beliefs that make up Christianity have not stayed static over the years, but they have moved and adapted throughout Christian history. The idea that the theology of the early church is the same as the ideas of theology in the USA today is not congruent. Wyman furthers this idea with the following analogy that likens theology to that of a building:

> In order for that structure [theology] to remain standing and to be a place that can stand up to new eventualities and crises it becomes necessary, in the eyes of constructive theology, to employ new materials in new configurations that not only

recognize but embrace the new technologies available that can ensure a structure that will withstand ...[37]

Declaring your theology to be fluid and not based in one historical or methodological understanding means that you will automatically be assumed to be 'contextual'. This automatically means that Practical Theology as theology that is human construction will be seen as a fringe theology by dogmatic or systematic theologians. In some ways, this works well for the project at hand, because those who are constructing theology here are doing so in a self-serving or bad way. This leads us, then, to a discussion of how one might identify 'good' or 'bad' constructions of Practical Theology.

Notes

1 Kathryn Tanner, *Theories of Culture: A New Agenda For Theology* (Minneapolis, MN: Augsburg Press, 1997), p. 93.

2 See Zoë Bennett, Elaine Graham, Stephen Pattison and Heather Walton, *Invitation to Research in Practical Theology* (Abingdon: Routledge, 2018).

3 See Richard Osmer, *Practical Theology: An Introduction* (Grand Rapids, MI: William B. Eerdmans, 2008), p. 11. Or Don Browning, *A Fundamental Practical Theology* (Minneapolis, MN: Fortress Press, 1995), pp. 1–9.

4 Jason Wyman Jr, *Constructing Constructive Theology: An Introductory Sketch* (Minneapolis, MN: Fortress Press, 2017), p. ix.

5 Wyman Jr, *Constructing Constructive Theology*, p. xvi.

6 Paul Tillich, *Systematic Theology, Vol. 1* (Chicago, IL: University of Chicago Press, 1951), p. 8.

7 Herbert Alden Youtz, 'Current Essays in Constructive Theology', *American Journal of Theology* 11.4 (October 1907), p. 694.

8 Wyman Jr, *Constructing Constructive Theology*, p. xxx.

9 Wyman Jr, *Constructing Constructive Theology*, pp. xxx–xxxi (my italics).

10 Gordon Kaufman, *The Theological Imagination* (Philadelphia, PA: Westminster Press, 1981), p. 263.

11 Kaufman, *The Theological Imagination*, p. 21.

12 Kaufman, *The Theological Imagination*, p. 21.

13 Kaufman, *The Theological Imagination*, p. 23.
14 Kaufman, *The Theological Imagination*, p. 27.
15 Kaufman, *The Theological Imagination*, p. 35.
16 Kaufman, *The Theological Imagination*, pp. 92–3.
17 Kaufman, *The Theological Imagination*, p. 89.
18 Kaufman, *The Theological Imagination*, p. 94.
19 Kaufman, *The Theological Imagination*, p. 94.
20 Kaufman, *The Theological Imagination*, p. 263.
21 Kathryn Tanner, *Theories of Culture: A New Agenda for Theology* (Minneapolis, MN: Fortress Press, 1997).
22 Tanner, *Theories of Culture*, p. 63.
23 Tanner, *Theories of Culture*, p. 65.
24 Tanner, *Theories of Culture*, p. 66.
25 Tanner, *Theories of Culture*, p. 76.
26 Tanner, *Theories of Culture*, p. 71.
27 Tanner, *Theories of Culture*, p. 70.
28 Tanner, *Theories of Culture*, p. 156.
29 Tanner, *Theories of Culture*, p. 155 (my italics).
30 Tanner, *Theories of Culture*, p. 171.
31 Tanner, *Theories of Culture*, p. 171.
32 Tanner, *Theories of Culture*, p. 171.
33 Tanner, *Theories of Culture*, p. 173.
34 Tanner, *Theories of Culture*, p. 174.
35 Tanner, *Theories of Culture*, p. 174.
36 Wyman Jr, *Constructing Constructive Theology*, p. xxxii.
37 Wyman Jr, *Constructing Constructive Theology*, p. xxxiii.

3

The Theological Task: 'Bad' and 'Good' Theology

Good theology needs to be a theology that takes risks. Good theology always needs to be humble, aware that no theology can say it all and that contexts are ever-changing.[1] (Stephen Bevans)

Christian Theology entered the New World of North and South America *diseased in form* and *distorted in performance*.[2] (Willie James Jennings)

Definitions

One of the key elements of this book is defining what constitutes 'good' and 'bad' Practical Theology. At the heart of this distinction lies the potential for a deep degree of bias that can occur when making such distinctions. The hope with presenting definitions in relation to good and bad is to establish a precedent by which those who create and who evaluate Practical Theology might be able to critique theology as good or bad with criteria that are shared by other scholars. Attempting to categorize religious beliefs in this way is difficult because of the subjective nature of that which is seen as being good and bad at a given time and in a given context. One book that has attempted to categorize this type of distinction is Peter Vardy's *Good and Bad Religion*.[3] In his text, Vardy outlines his reasoning behind declaring various religions as good or bad. His disclaimer is one that this book also incorporates:

This book continues a debate that has been going on at some level for millennia, yet which is bound to fail. My hope is that in failing it may serve to revive discussion of the central question, promote evaluation of the things people do in the name of faith and encourage action by motivating individuals and groups to stand out against aspects of their own religious traditions that need to be challenged and condemned.[4]

Accordingly, the goal for my project is not simply to present theology that I, as the author, do not like. Instead, the hope is to bring together criteria that share common characteristics of theology that can be damaging or oppressive. The idea is that if this characterization can occur then it might encourage discussion about, as Vardy states, 'the things people do in the name of faith'.[5] As someone who comes from 'inside' the Christian faith, I am hoping that this will cause some self-critique from those of us who are hoping for continued reflection and renewal within Christianity in the face of a changing society and world.

What, then, are Vardy's ideas around that which is deemed good and bad? He begins his text by stating that inevitably his distinguishing of religions as either good or bad will be controversial. He is also quick to say that he is absolutely not trying to write a book about which *religions* are good or bad. Instead, his goal is to try to establish 'criteria by which some manifestations of religion (which may be found within any or all traditions) may be described in these terms'.[6] He does not claim to be doing anything new by looking at these manifestations of religion; instead, he believes that he is participating in an ongoing debate that has been in existence for many years. People have, throughout history, criticized aspects of religion (practices or otherwise). Vardy in this sense is simply looking to systematize and analyse these criticisms.

He acknowledges that part of the controversy surrounding the analysis of religious practice is the idea of people being hesitant to criticize their own religion. Those who belong to a religious group are often unwilling to challenge their own religion from within. There is a fear of being ostracized from the group, but there are also wider implications from a faith perspective. Most religious people feel as though their beliefs are absolute truth, and that the interpretations of the texts within the group are the accurate conclusions. As a result, religious groups will often serve as self-justifying institutions that base their justification on divinity. This is not the space to debate the truth behind any claims to divine connection; Vardy simply wants to offer insights into why people do not tend to critique their own religious institutions. His conclusion is that people often falter in the face of peer pressure in a community's self-justifying divine conclusions. As a result of this self-justification, most religions do not acknowledge critique from inside their community and certainly not from outside. Religions believe they have God-knowledge, or theology, and as a result if anything from outside of their own interpretations challenges their knowledge it is quickly rejected. This lack of reflection is problematic on many different levels. Most predominant is the idea that the self-justification of religious communities means that there is little room for analysis of beliefs or actions.

Accordingly, Vardy establishes two criteria in relation to the tendencies towards the self-justification of religion. First, there is no independent standard of goodness by which God's actions can be judged in a universal way. Therefore, there is no way of knowing objectively if something is commanded by God or supposed to be commanded by God. This is one reason why, Vardy claims, judging religions as good or bad can be problematic if a group believes that their religion has come straight from God. He doesn't believe, however, that this means that the project of good and bad religious actions in the world is dead. Vardy understands that there have to be other means by which one can discuss religious belief as good or bad. He states: 'if the commands of a religion differ markedly from what most moral philosophies would argue to be good actions, this could be a starting point from which to judge those commands.'[7] While there is a wide selection of 'moral philosophies' and, indeed, interpretations of these philosophies, Vardy has limited his criteria for judgement to a few key areas, and focuses on the idea of life-giving theologies within religion as being the main criterion for good religion. He offers the following: 'On this view, religion is about helping individuals to fulfil their true potential to become what they are capable of being at their very best. Actions are wrong that diminish us and lead us away from our potential that all human beings share.'[8] This idea of human flourishing as the goal of human life is shared in various ways by philosophers such as Kant and Aquinas, according to Vardy.

Vardy acknowledges that this outside perspective might not be adequate as an authority of what is good and bad for people who are religious. This is because most religions have a sacred text that they see as being the ultimate 'to do list' with regard to their actions in the world. The problem with using the texts as the means by which one lives, or indeed attempts to live in a good way, is that they are complicated at best. Vardy offers the following:

> The Bible has been used to justify slavery, apartheid, the suppression of women, the 'evils' of sexuality, the 'evils' of homosexuality, a male-only priesthood, the denial of any priests at all, the supremacy of the Pope, the irrelevance of the Pope, the authority of the Church, a denial of the authority of the Church, a feminist agenda, war, pacifism and almost any other position that people may wish to hold.[9]

Texts are not analysed in a vacuum. There is a construction that occurs when people are involved in reading and creating theological conclusions. Many religious people will argue that there is divine intervention in translations, or that scholars are interpreting the literal meaning of a text. The issue with both of these perspectives is that the vast number of varying translations of the same text conflict with these understandings. The idea of translation of texts is at the centre of Vardy's discussion of good and bad religion, not only in the interpretation of texts with regard to theological conclusion as was stated in his quote, but the openness that religions have to discuss their conclusions with people who disagree with them. Good religion, according to Vardy, will be open to these discussions. Religious groups will not close themselves off to other interpretations of a text just because they contradict their own views. Vardy states: 'This is one of the most fundamental ways of distinguishing good from bad religion – whether a religion can recognize at least the possibility of its error.'[10] He sees one of the major errors of bad religion being people holding the view that their conclusions are without error because they come from God. By looking at the varying (and harmful) ways the texts have been translated, one can see how differing accounts of the same text can be dangerous.

Another area that Vardy sees as being important to those who are practising good religion is the pursuit of justice. Justice, he says, is at the centre of good religion. Unfortunately, the question will inevitably arise about the nature of justice. In other words, whose justice is the right justice? Again, Vardy turns to philosophers – namely, Immanuel Kant – to help distinguish what is justice from what is injustice. According to Vardy:

> Justice requires dispassionate, rational analysis. It requires seeing both sides of a case. It is directly related to fairness. Justice may not always be easily discernible, but where people of good will can put aside self-interest it should be achievable and recognizable.[11]

The consequences of not pursuing justice in relation to religious practice can have catastrophic consequences. Vardy offers examples from the Holocaust, whereby members of the Christian churches stood by and were silent while grave injustice occurred around them. This, he says, is an example of bad religion; that is, when the institution becomes more important than the pursuit of justice. He also mentions people who state that they are doing justice in the name of God's will, but in fact are doing severe injustice. This is another key area of bad religion according to Vardy.

A final area of judging good and bad religion offered by Vardy is related to areas of equality and freedom. With regard to equality, he gives as examples: slavery as a form of oppression should never be tolerated; people should be treated with respect; groups of people should not be ostracized based on their existence; people should have freedoms that allow them to pursue activities for human flourishing; and people should be paid according to the work they do. A main reason why these basic ideas of equality must be discussed in relation to good and bad religion is that traditionally religions have not necessarily pursued an agenda of equality in their practices. For example, Christianity and Islam are both guilty of accepting the institution of slavery. Hinduism has also accepted the caste system in India, which is a form of social oppression. Furthermore, women have often been treated as less than men in certain religious traditions.

Equality is closely related to the field of ethics in many religious traditions. In other words, the pursuit of equality in a variety of forms can be filtered through the religious texts and traditions of communities in order to reach social conclusions. Recent practical examples of this in the Christian faith include women being denied ordination in certain churches, the anti-abortion agenda or condemning the LGBTQ community. These examples are based on theological conclusions of certain Christian groups, and the opinions of these groups are not shared across the entire Christian population. Vardy is not interested in debating these ethical conclusions of certain religious traditions; instead he wants to move the conversation towards alternative understandings of what 'good' constitutes with regard to equality. Good religion is not a religion that holds a certain view, Vardy argues, but instead:

> reference may be made to the way in which religions engage in ethical debate and whether this is done in a spirit of openness to alternative views, with humility and compassion and, per-

haps above all, with respect and an attempt at understanding for people having to wrestle with hard ethical decisions.[12]

Vardy is quick to point out that this does not mean there are no ethical absolutes, but simply that good religion is open to discussing a variety of alternatives when it comes to ethical conclusions, especially in relation to equality. These discussions must take place because of the way equality has been historically stifled in the context of religious practice.

Freedom is the final criterion that Vardy says is necessary for a religion to be considered good. Freedom means multiple things within the context of religion, but fundamentally it directly relates to the idea of human flourishing. People should have the freedom to choose their religion, and to choose the religious beliefs that help them to flourish in the world. Accordingly, they should not be forced into religious practice via fear or intimidation, but instead should be able to make choices with regard to their religion and practices. Vardy says that this freedom is often limited in religions as they become institutionalized because their institutionalization means that rules and regulations (or rites and rituals) become hard-and-fast rules for those who are part of a certain religious community. Freedom to manoeuvre in that religious space becomes increasingly difficult as the institutional religion attempts to maintain its place – and ultimately its power – in the world. According to Vardy: 'Bad religion has forgotten that religion is at least partly a human invention – a human response to a mystery that is never more than partially understood.'[13]

Ultimately, Vardy offers insights into what can be viewed as good and bad religious practices. These criteria are related to religious sacred texts (and their interpretations), science and religion (or the positive view of science by religion), the pursuit of justice and equality, and finally the understanding of freedoms within the context of religion. Vardy understands what he is undertaking with regard to his criteria of good and bad, and also admits his own bias as he goes through the text. His conclusions, though, are helpful for my project. People are afraid to declare that something is good or bad in relation to religion, but by using philosophy and practical historical examples, Vardy is able to reach conclusions about good and bad instances in religion (as opposed to condemning an entire religious group). Ultimately, Vardy defines good religious practice as, first: 'Any religion must aim to foster human flourishing, to help human beings develop their full potential, however this may be defined', and second, 'that human beings must be genuinely free to make choices without being wholly determined'.[14] While one might disagree with his conclusions, his criteria are helpful for openly debating the actions of certain religious groups at certain times in history.

Having a definitive list of what constitutes good and bad is not Vardy's intention. He is, instead, interested in opening up a previously avoided discussion about the times when religions have not acted in a way that would constitute good religion. The point of bringing attention to these instances in history, and noting what made various religions behave badly, means that we can take this knowledge forward to try and address these issues in future religious practice. It also allows people to have agency when it comes to addressing areas within their own tradition that they believe to be examples of bad religious practice. This type of challenge by people within a religious community should be a means by which conversations can occur about religious practice, and should not result in a typecasting, shunning or exclusion. Another academic, Duncan Ferguson, discusses this idea of good and bad religion from a spirituality point of view. His views are reflected in the following sections.

Spirituality as 'life-affirming' and 'life-denying'[15]

Duncan Ferguson, former Professor of Religious Studies at Eckerd College in the USA, offers a similar criterion for good and bad religion. In his book *Exploring the Spirituality of the World Religions*, Ferguson analyses spiritual practices and spirituality from a wide variety of religious traditions. One of his framing chapters for this exploration involves considering the differences between what he calls 'life-affirming' and 'life-denying' spirituality. Ferguson begins his discussion by admitting his bias as a Protestant Christian who is writing in the year 2010. As a result, he sees affirming and denying spirituality through his own personal, historical lens. That being said, Ferguson believes that a list of life-denying and life-affirming characteristics of spirituality should exist, and that this list should be continuously evolving and adjusted according to the time and place in which it is being employed.

 Ferguson offers an excellent backdrop as to why he wanted to write his particular text. As he studied religion across the globe, he began to notice two central ideas. Religions, and indeed spiritual or theological practices, were capable of creating very positive – and, equally, incredibly negative – situations for people. He writes: 'It struck me that religious faith can be enormously powerful in human experience, lead to health, human flourishing, and social responsibility, but also it can lead to an orientation of fear, zealotry, and intolerance.'[16] As Ferguson travelled the world, he began to make lists of characteristics that he saw in different religions that constituted life-giving and life-denying aspects of their beliefs and practices. The life-denying characteristics can often lead to people leaving a religious tradition. They can also lead to a closed-off fundamentalism, as described by Ferguson. On the other hand, he believes that life-giving spirituality can increase tolerance and help people to better understand ideas like peace, justice and reconciliation.[17] He adds:

My experience, observations and study of religious life coupled with the rise of spirituality and fundamentalism have led me to the conviction that religious beliefs and practices and their expression in spirituality are shaping contemporary life in quite profound ways.[18]

According to Ferguson, there are five characteristics of both life-giving and life-denying spirituality. A life-giving spirituality is one that empowers people to live lives that add value to the society in which they live, through living with understanding and compassion. It guides a group or a person in a life that is looking to make the world a better place. It does not align itself exclusively with political groups or other agencies that wield power. There is an openness in life-giving spirituality that means that people who follow it are open to other beliefs and opinions. There is a self-reflection of the spirituality in an intellectual way. The followers of life-giving spirituality flourish in their society. Finally, life-giving spirituality helps a group or an individual to get through difficult times. It is a spirituality that sustains those who follow it.

Life-denying spirituality is characterized by its closed-off nature. First, it is closed to other religious points of view. There is judgement of others who adhere to different spiritualities or religions. There is suspicion of people who are unlike you in your beliefs. There is a lack of intellectual self-criticism in relation to the spirituality; instead, there is blanket acceptance of beliefs and practices. This spirituality is characterized by its overzealous nature. There is a desire for everyone to believe in this life-denying spirituality, and sometimes by using violent means to achieve this. Life-denying spirituality has a susceptibility to being used by political groups or by people in power. Such spirituality demonstrates an 'If you aren't with us, you are against us' mentality. This means that there is a great deal of 'fear, mistrust and intolerance and [the spiritual pathway] does not reflect the positive values of personal transformation, compassion, justice, and peace'.[19] These characteristics offered by Ferguson further help one to identify that which is considered good or bad religion or, in Ferguson's words, life-giving or life-denying spirituality. As we move to discussing specific examples of bad Practical Theology, I want to keep in mind the very similar criteria offered by both Vardy and Ferguson in relation to distinguishing the practice of theology that is devoted to human flourishing and openness and that which is not. This will help us all to be able to identify bad or life-denying Practical Theology.

Recognizing bad Practical Theology: my methods

> Theology is not merely a repetition of the Word of God in a vacuum but a reflection on God's Word in relation to contemporary realities. Theology is thus simultaneously engaged in two related quests. It is a quest for an understanding of the various Biblical doctrines within a particular culture and a questioning of that culture in terms of Biblical faith.[20]

As we come to the end of Part I of this book, I want to bring together the methodological aspects of the research that I have been laying out in Chapters 1—3. First and foremost, my project is one that situates itself under the umbrella of Practical Theology. The methodology is firmly a Practical Theology endeavour, and as a result I will be incorporating research methods from Practical Theology.

But what makes this project a Practical Theology one? To answer this question, we will examine the primary theses of this book:

1 Theology is a human construct.
2 Theology is fundamentally Practical Theology.
3 Practical Theology is thus a human construct.
4 One of the key tasks of Practical Theology is to be able to identify *what is going on* in constructed theology in the contemporary world.
5 Another key task of Practical Theology is identifying what this constructed theology *should be*.
6 What constructed Practical Theology *should be* in the world can be identified by analysing theological conclusions against criteria that identify both good and bad religion and/or life-giving and life-denying spirituality.

7 This analysis can be done via qualitative research methods (based on the criteria offered) or through analysis of historical case studies based on practical theological reflection (based on the criteria offered).

From the beginning, Practical Theology has started from the assumption that theology is a human construction. The founding father of Practical Theology, Friedrich Schleiermacher, believed that theology could be studied as a human endeavour. And perhaps even more importantly, he believed that Practical Theology was firmly based in a particular time and place. Don Browning took this idea and developed it further by saying that all theology is fundamentally Practical Theology. This understanding was based on the belief that any theology that looked like theory alone had ultimately been abstracted from practice. Browning also gave credit to communities of religious believers as creators of theological wisdom. He saw these communities as being able to communicate practical reason with regard to their belief systems, despite not always coming to 'good' conclusions. Browning believes that this is simply the way that theology is developed in the world. People always have bias in the way they process information, but if they can identify and reflect on that bias in theology it can be a helpful developmental exercise. They can discuss their bias and beliefs and take these thoughts back to the texts; this can lead to practice, and then the process begins again. Practical Theology, in this way, is reflected in Woodward and Pattison's definition: 'Practical Theology is concerned with actions, issues and events that are of human significance in the contemporary world.'

Why is there a disconnect between what theology is and what theology should be? Kathryn Tanner believes that theology is ultimately God working in the world, but that it still remains a human production. As a result, culture can influence that which is produced on behalf of God. Gordon Kaufman defines the difference between what *is* and what *should be* through his understanding of God and 'reality God'. Reality God is that which God does in the world; the constructed God is the one that humans hope God to be in the world. A complete understanding of reality God is unattainable to finite beings, according to Kaufman, and as a result the constructed God is what we see presented in theology. How, then, do people know what is from reality God and what is not? According to Kaufman, this is an impossible task, but there are ways to analyse how much of theology is coming from a negative human construction as opposed to a positive one.

As a result of this focus on a negative construction of God, some scholars have begun researching the means by which people might refer to a religion as positive or negative in a given time or context. Peter Vardy and Duncan Forrester have both created criteria using which one might analyse what is good or bad religion, and what is life-affirming or life-denying. When analysed together, Vardy's criteria and Forrester's criteria are strikingly similar. I have assembled these criteria in combined lists below:[21]

'Good' theology

1 Your theology must relate to human flourishing. This inevitably will be defined in different ways, but people should feel as though their theology sustains, guides and promotes them in their given context.
2 There must be space in your theology to self-reflect both at a personal level and at a community level.
3 Your theology should be open to hearing about the thoughts and beliefs of others even if they are different from your own thoughts and beliefs.
4 Alongside the openness to others, there should be freedom when it comes to an individual choosing their own theology.
5 There should be an openness to pursue justice in your theology. While this will look different depending on your context, there should exist in your theology a desire to liberate those who are oppressed.

6 Alongside this pursuit of justice, there should also be a desire for equality, both within one's tradition and outside in the secular world.

'Bad' theology

1 Your theology is used to limit people's flourishing. This will inevitably be defined in different ways, but those oppressed under bad theology may feel they are not properly guided, sustained or promoted in their given context.
2 There is little or no self-reflection in your theology. Instead, there is judgement on those who do not share the same theology.
3 There is no desire within your theology to interact with those who are outside your own community. In fact, there is an us versus them mentality when it comes to those who don't believe as you do.
4 Your theology is isolated from the rest of the world or from others who have a different theology from yours. Those within your community have little or no choice in theology.
5 There is no desire for justice in the wider world in your theology, unless that justice fits within the already existing belief systems of your community.
6 There is no desire for equality in the wider world, unless that equality fits within already existing belief systems of your community.

As has been previously discussed, Practical Theology can be researched in the contemporary world through a variety of methods, and these methods are increasingly how scholars define the type of Practical Theology they are doing. If we are looking to distinguish Practical Theology as good or bad, the use of these criteria is the start of this analysis. One means of doing research in this way is by undertaking qualitative research in order to observe or interview people who are doing Practical Theology in a given context. Another means of analysing good/ bad Practical Theology is by looking at historical examples.

The four historical, theological case studies being analysed in this book are:

- Chapter 4: Apartheid in South Africa: A Bad Theology of Providence
- Chapter 5: John Winthrop and John Mason: A Bad Theology of Election
- Chapter 6: The History of the Ku Klux Klan: A Bad Theology of Tradition
- Chapter 7: The Massacre at Jonestown: A Bad Theology of Eschatology

Each of these chapters begins with a discussion of the traditional, systematic idea that I argue was used as a means of perpetuating bad theology in the given context of the chapter. As a result, I will include a brief word here about the systematic content in question. In *The Oxford Handbook of Systematic Theology*,[22] John Webster calls this type of activity the 'theological task'. Following many of the theologians mentioned thus far in this book, Webster talks about the idea that theology is constructed and therefore needs to be examined and scrutinized as a result. He says: 'To make a representation of Christian teaching is to construe it, to commend a version of it which may not be made up but is certainly made. This, in turn, reinforces the need for criteria against which the adequacy of systematic construals can be assessed.'[23] However, in light of the idea that theology is constructed, Webster still defends systematic theology as vital to the overall understanding of the Christian tradition. In my opinion, he is being quite generous in his views on the practicality of systematic theology. He is also quick to defend systematics against the prevailing attitude held by Practical Theologians that systematic theology is simply abstracted theology. Webster and I shall remain in our respective corners on this issue.

Webster believes that concepts such as trinity, election, providence are all important because they look to organize certain repeated scriptural ideas in the Christian text. Not only are these fundamental concepts, according to systematics, but they are ones that offer further contemplation to Christians in the world. The South African theologian Charles Villa-Vicencio calls such concepts 'usable Christianity' and warns that these themes can be adapted and adjusted to fit someone's view of the world. He states: 'The Biblical message is trimmed and cropped until it fits the frame which has been decided, and the result is that the eagle (with his clipped wings) can no long rise and fly away to his true element but can be pointed out as a special showpiece among the other animals.'[24] Villa-Vicencio warns that once this manipulation of theology can no longer be used to justify a Christian concept, it is discarded. At that stage, by all accounts, the concept no longer needs the justification because it has become the understood norm on a given subject.

Even Webster admits that the concepts of systematic theology can be historical and historically justified by those who benefit from it. He also states that the demands of what he says are 'pastoral' or 'apologetic' occasions can mean that Christian doctrine can be led into 'distortion'.[25] Villa-Vicencio confirms this by saying:

> As [Karl] Barth never tired of reminding us, apart from and without Jesus Christ we can say nothing at all about God and [humanity]. Yet it is also the task of theology to reflect on the truth made known in Christ, to distinguish the true from the false, and not only to stammer before the truth but to speak.[26]

My understanding of this conclusion is that by the words 'pastoral' and 'apologetic' Webster means the forms by which Christian theology can become Practical Theology. Again, this is a very generous view of systematics, but he goes on to say: 'Under pressure from such demands, doctrines can expand or contract, or can be made to serve purposes for which they were not intended.'[27] Webster does reflect on the systematic task when he says that the real question of making a system of theology is about how far the human brain can actually go in terms of creating and understanding that which is divine: 'Systematic schematization may neglect the mind's fallibility and the provisionality of its representations ... systematic representation may mischaracterize the object of Christian teaching, especially when that "object" is considered to be the personal communicative presence and activity of God.'[28]

Webster very much emphasizes that many theologians have questioned the systematic task, even the big man himself, Karl Barth. Webster concludes that 'no representation of Christian teaching can attain a fully determinate rendering of the topic; aspirations can be fulfilled only by reduction or selection.'[29] All is not lost for the systematic theology task, however, and Webster does believe that there are appropriate means by which theology can be organized. His version of this type of theological task focuses on the who and what of God; the relation of God to the world; systems that fit with tradition and do not attempt to replace that which is established as Christian teaching; and the need for some form of scope and coherence. These are summaries, of course, and the reader can check out the exact criteria of the systematic theology task in Webster's writing. I felt it important, though, to show that there are means by which even the systematic theologians are working to try and establish criteria by which they can evaluate the abstract concepts that continue to prove important to the theological task.

This book will use the systematic theological concepts that are held dear by the Christian tradition in order to show how they have been manipulated into something that was 'not as it was intended', as Webster states. My criteria are different from Webster's, and to some extent that is because I am evaluating from a practical theological point of view. That being said, it is a good foundation to know that even systematic theologians have felt nervous about the way that certain concepts are used as a complete understanding of the divine. This claim to a complete knowledge is the practical theological task at hand. Because some leaders have presented certain concepts as complete and set in stone, many people have regarded what they said as being right, true and good, even when it was justifying some of the world's greatest evils.

Alongside my criteria for bad theology, Richard Osmer's practical theological methods will be used in organizing Chapters 4 to 7 and in each case study. To review, the tasks (methods) are as follows:

1 Descriptive-empirical task
2 Interpretative task
3 Normative task
4 Pragmatic task.[30]

The descriptive-empirical task of each case study will involve giving the history/background for the particular context. The interpretative task will include analysing the theological conclusions of each case study with the criteria of good and bad Practical Theology. The normative task will involve naming the theological conclusions that fall within bad Practical Theology in each case study, and further discussions will take place about how these bad Practical Theology conclusions came to be. The normative task will also look at how these case studies serve as examples of bad Practical Theology as opposed to good Practical Theology. The pragmatic task is more difficult with regard to the case studies, as one cannot go back in time and stop the bad Practical Theology from happening; but there is a beneficial element in showing that these case studies do represent bad Practical Theology, and to name it as such. As a result, the pragmatic task for all of the case studies is simply having the conversation about each of them with the acknowledgement that these events could be repeated in the future if not recognized for what they are. When one is doing qualitative research within this methodological framework, there will be a clearer means by which pragmatic tasks might be able to start a conversation in a contemporary context to move towards practical change. It is with this methodology and criteria in hand that we move on to the case studies, all examples of what could be considered bad Practical Theology.

Notes

1 Stephen Bevans, 'Contextual Theology as Practical Theology' in *Opening the Field of Practical Theology*, ed. Kathleen A. Cahalan and Gordon S. Mikoski (Lanham, MD: Rowman & Littlefield, 2014), p. 58.

2 Willie James Jennings, 'Disfigurations of Christian Identity' in *Lived Theology*, ed. Charles Marsh, Peter Slade and Sarah Azaransky (Oxford: Oxford University Press, 2017), p. 67 (italics original).

3 Peter Vardy, *Good and Bad Religion* (London: SCM Press, 2010).

4 Vardy, *Good and Bad Religion*, p. viii.

5 Vardy, *Good and Bad Religion*, p. viii.

6 Vardy, *Good and Bad Religion*, p. vii.

7 Vardy, *Good and Bad Religion*, p. 49.

8 Vardy, *Good and Bad Religion*, p. 62.

9 Vardy, *Good and Bad Religion*, p. 79.

10 Vardy, *Good and Bad Religion*, p. 94.

11 Vardy, *Good and Bad Religion*, p. 135.

12 Vardy, *Good and Bad Religion*, p. 155.

13 Vardy, *Good and Bad Religion*, p. 167.

14 Vardy, *Good and Bad Religion*, p. 162.

15 Duncan Ferguson, *Exploring the Spirituality of the World Religions* (London: Continuum, 2010), p. 10.

16 Ferguson, *Exploring the Spirituality of the World Religions*, p. ix.

17 Ferguson, *Exploring the Spirituality of the World Religions*, p. xi.

18 Ferguson, *Exploring the Spirituality of the World Religions*, p. xii.

19 Ferguson, *Exploring the Spirituality of the World Religions*, p. 10.

20 Charles Villa-Vicencio, 'Theology and Politics in South Africa', *Journal of Theology for South Africa* 17 (1976), p. 25.

21 I am aware that there are semantic issues (and indeed disciplinary differences) between religion, spirituality and theology. My argument is that the criteria that are presented here are transferable in their nature when discussing theology.

22 John Webster, Kathryn Tanner and Iain Torrance, eds, *The Oxford Handbook of Systematic Theology* (Oxford: Oxford University Press, 2007).

23 John Webster, in *The Oxford Handbook of Systematic Theology*, p. 7.

24 Villa-Vicencio, 'Theology and Politics in South Africa', p. 26.

25 John Webster, in *The Oxford Handbook of Systematic Theology*, pp. 12–13.

26 Villa-Vicencio, 'Theology and Politics in South Africa', p. 25.

27 John Webster, in *The Oxford Handbook of Systematic Theology*, p. 13.

28 John Webster, in *The Oxford Handbook of Systematic Theology*, p. 13.

29 John Webster, in *The Oxford Handbook of Systematic Theology*, p. 14.

30 Richard Osmer, *Practical Theology: An Introduction* (Grand Rapids, MI: William B. Eerdmans, 2008), p. 4.

PART II

4

Apartheid in South Africa: A Bad Theology of Providence

Providence and theology

The systematic theological ideas around providence are some of the earliest we see in literature when considering the relationship between God and the created world. Providence asks the questions about God's involvement in the history of the world, and how we as humans might understand certain events that happen or do not happen in history. This was understandably one of the first questions that was asked by those who adhered to monotheistic religions because it was at the centre of any religious belief system. The Christian tradition knew that there must be ideas (and indeed rules) set up about just how little or how much God actually interacted with people, and also what these interactions said about the nature of God.

It was from these contemplations in the monotheistic traditions that we begin to see the idea of providence emerge. Christian thinkers interacted with Greco-Roman philosophers and adopted some of the ideas and conclusions they came to. According to Charles Wood: 'As the Christian movement began to seek and to gain religious legitimacy, it borrowed heavily from the religious philosophies accepted among the cultured elites of the Roman Empire, and the idea of providence was among the borrowings.'[1] This borrowing was quite common in the Roman Empire and surrounding regions. The exchanging of ideas between philosophers and religions was commonplace, as people were connected by the empire (even if not by culture or geography).

A particularly influential philosophy on early Christian thinkers was Stoicism. The ideas of the Stoics fit incredibly well with the teachings of Christianity, and as a result many Christian writers (including St Paul) took these ideas on board in order to further develop their own understanding of a very young Christian tradition. Stoic concepts – such as renouncing human wealth and status for contemplation and charity; liberation for all people regardless of status, gender, race or personal situation; and the idea that one needs to have a conversion experience to move away from worldly ways and attachments – were all very attractive to early Christians. There were some differences between the understanding of the Stoics and that of Christianity – for example, how we determine what is worldly – but the influence of these philosophers on systematic theology cannot be denied.

Some scholars of history might ask why the theology of providence was so important for the early church, and consequently for Christianity as it continued moving forward in history. The understanding that God was working in the world on the side of believers was, and remains, a key element of the Christian tradition. The extent to which God is working, or not working, is where the debates began to roll in. From the early church to the Reformation, some of the foundational theologians in the Christian tradition debated the means by which God interacted with humanity, as well as the events of the world. The theologian David Fergusson traces the history of providence in Christian history in his article 'The Theology of Providence'.[2] He explains that the early church took a lot of ideas about providence from philosophers, as has been mentioned. The idea that the gods had a great deal to do with human affairs was always a common theme in the Greco-Roman world. Almost from the beginning there was tension in the adoption of some of these ideas into the Christian world. Does God determine *everything*, down to the very planetary movements and the seasons? Or does God have a plan, but is inherently influenced by human actions and earthly events? Or is there some sort of deist understanding whereby God has little to do with earth and was just the clock-maker that set the world in motion and then walked away? These are merely some of the arguments that took place in the early church about the role of God's providence in the world.

The theologians of the Reformation led the discussion away from questioning and more towards the sovereignty of God, and God's ultimate control over the world. The questioning over God's intervention in worldly events 'collapse'[3] in the Reformation. God becomes a determinist choir director in the eyes of these theologians. Also, God becomes someone who is working out the world and worldly events in favour of those who follow the Christian tradition. There are some important issues with this, according to Fergusson: 'While this is moving and appealing in many ways, it suggests too hastily that everything works out well in the best of all possible worlds. In some future estate, there will be a perspective by which our seeming misfortunes are rendered blessings.'[4]

Fergusson, and other theologians who have analysed this particularly contentious theological concept, have many issues with the conclusions that have been drawn on the topic of providence. One of the last concerns expressed in the article 'The Theology of Providence' is:

A further reason for a greater caution than is apparent in many speculative accounts of providence is our awareness of the ways in which these too readily have been co-opted for imperialist and totalitarian projects ... Within the rhetoric of these political regimes, there were powerful but problematic claims to be the vehicles in world history of divine providence.[5]

It is this problematic vehicle that has crashed through the likes of the USA, Northern Ireland and Israel–Palestine. For this discussion, though, we look at how it has affected South Africa.

A religious history of South Africa

On the one hand, the [Afrikaner] clergy strongly favored racial segregation and economic discrimination against non-whites ... Yet, on the other hand, they had to deal with Christianity's doctrine of the equality of all persons before the Almighty. Much ingenious theology was the result, of the sort that reminds one of the suggestion that the real purpose of most theology is to make excuses for the behavior of both God and man.[6]

To begin a Christian, religious history of South Africa, we have to begin with the first missionaries/colonists who came from Europe to the continent of Africa. I say missionary/colonists because there has been a long history of debates as to what constitutes the differences between colonists and missionaries. That particular debate won't be discussed here. That is simply because I do not see the distinction as making much of a difference to the overall conclusions that I am trying to draw. Ultimately there were people from Europe who came to South Africa for a variety of reasons, one of which was missionary work.

The first Europeans we see arriving in South Africa were the Dutch in 1652, followed by the French Huguenots in 1668. German colonists followed soon after. Overwhelmingly, these first colonists were Protestant in background. The Dutch Reformed Church (DRC), famous for its work in South Africa, was the predominant church in the early days of colonialization in South Africa. They were known in Dutch and Afrikaans as the Nederduitse Gereformeerde Kerk (NGK). Despite the predominance of Protestant, Dutch influence in the Cape colonies during this time, mission work was not the main focus in the eighteenth century. There was a growing number of missionaries in the NGK church, but these were mostly drawn from the population of white settlers at the time. The first significant missionary movement in the area occurred via the Moravians in 1738. Under George Schmidt, the Moravian church led an intense missionary outreach to the local, indigenous South African people.[7] Unfortunately for Schmidt, the theology of the Moravian church was in opposition to a lot of the theological concepts of the prevailing NGK settler church – namely, the idea of universal grace and salvation that the Moravian church preached, which was in contradiction to the Calvinistic ideas around predestination and God's role in salvation.[8]

From the beginning, there was clearly a great deal of difference between what was considered the 'settler' church and the 'missionary' church. By the time the British gained control of the Cape colonies in the nineteenth century, this conflict had come to a head. The churches of the NGK pushed back against the missionary churches, who were trying to convert indigenous people to Christianity. Members of the NGK did not see the need for the South African people to be Christians; in fact, they were 'unconvinced about the need for and desirability of such missionary enthusiasm and endeavour'.[9]

By 1824, two major events had affected the NGK church in South Africa. One was that the British had officially taken control of the Cape colonies. The second was that the NGK had broken free from its Dutch roots and become independent. In fact, it was the future Independent Christian Church in South Africa. Therefore, on the one hand the NGK was free from control (both administratively and theologically) by its European counterpart, but it was controlled by the Anglican-leaning rule of the British empire. It is worth noting at this stage that despite the NGK breaking free from the connection to the Dutch church, there was little by way of a unified theological understanding even in the NGK church in South Africa (connection to Europe or not). While many who read the history of South Africa assume that the NGK had strong Calvinist roots that guided the people of that particular denomination, the reality was less organized and certainly less unified. According to the historian Donald Akenson: 'What we do not find is a people [Afrikaners] with an agreed sense of mission. We do not find a social group that believes it is a Chosen People. We do not find "Calvinism" in the sloppy, generalized sense of the word.'[10] If the theology of Calvin was not the driving force among Afrikaners, then what was their main community-forming theology? The answer is the Old Testament. There was a complete lack of Christology in these early interpretations of the Bible by Afrikaners. In fact, in some circles, the Christian texts that focused on equality and freedom were largely ignored. Akenson states: 'This means that the distorting lens that Christianity places in front of the Hebrew texts was removed, and that the Afrikaner people of the first two-thirds of the nineteenth century encouraged unmediated the covenantal grid of the ancient Hebrews.'[11]

What did this covenantal grid mean for Afrikaners during this time? It meant that God had preferential treatment for the Afrikaners. This included the belief that Afrikaners were the rightful owners of the land that God had provided for them – South Africa in particular. The feeling among Afrikaners was the idea that their blood had been shed for this land, the land God intended for them, and as a result they were the rightful heirs. Alongside the need for the land that God intended, the Afrikaners also had a strong sense of history that tied them to this land. According to Akenson: 'The Afrikaners thought historically, not in the same way that historians might, but they used history as the ancient Hebrews did, to explain the past in moral terms and to guide their planning for the future.'[12] It was the Hebrew texts, and specifically the story of the Israelites and their covenant with God (both in protection and in land), that brought together the disparate theological views of the Afrikaner people.

Despite the feeling of community that came with the Hebrew stories of overcoming adversity and the importance of the land, there was always the threat of the British empire on the cultural world of the Afrikaners. Despite both being European, fundamentally the Afrikaners viewed the British, ironically, as a foreign, colonial force in the region. This was seen especially when the British abolished slavery in 1833 in the colonies. Not only was abolishing slavery viewed as a slap economically for the Afrikaners, but it was also seen as a lack of understanding of God's will when it comes to the order of humanity. The Afrikaners were not only a chosen people, they also firmly believed that there was an order to the universe. An order that God had established for all creation.

The abolition of slavery confirmed to the Afrikaners that the British were clueless about their way of life. The British had also passed several laws that focused on excluding non-English speakers from positions of power and from owning businesses. It was a true clash of cultures where neither side was willing to find a meaningful middle ground. And so they did what a great number of groups have historically done when they cannot resolve their differences. They moved away from one another. The Afrikaners began what has historically been called 'The Great Trek'. Again, this story is shrouded in myth and as a result the details are sketchy at best, but what is known is that a large group of Afrikaners left the Cape area in order to escape British rule. The 'Voortrekkers', as they were later named, were searching for land away from the Cape, in order to set up their community in an area that was more friendly to their way of life. As the Voortrekkers made their way into the wilderness, they were reading the Hebrew texts and likening their experience to that of the Israelites:

> As they journeyed, the pages came alive with meaning and relevance. The exodus of the people of Israel and their testing in the wilderness were happening again. Any obstacle along the way to the promised land had to be overcome, by sheer grit and by the gun. Any doubt of divine providence was not only unthinkable, but blasphemy, a harbinger of disaster. The church at the Cape was no longer relevant, but the saga of Israel in the holy book was.[13]

In 1838, the Voortrekkers arrived in Zulu territory. The result was not peaceful, and nearly 300 Afrikaners were ambushed and killed by the Zulu. In retaliation, in 1838, 200 Voortrekkers fought the Zulu warriors. This time, the Voortrekkers killed more than 3,000 Zulu at the Battle of Blood River. No

Afrikaners were killed in this battle – a battle that is of massive importance to the overall providential narrative of the Afrikaners in South Africa. It also led to a splitting of the Afrikaners' churches in the region, as increasing tensions about racial relations began to take over theological discussions. The result was three separate white Afrikaner Reformed churches: the NGK, the Nederduitsch Hervormde Kerk (NHK), a church established by the Voortrekkers, and the Gereformeerde Kerk (GK). The Voortrekkers took covenantal oaths at Blood Creek as a result of their victory. They reaffirmed their commitment to God, and the knowledge that God was working to their greater end. The Battle of Blood Creek became a point of remembrance for the Afrikaners, 16 December marking a yearly celebration of the Voortrekkers' defeat of the Zulu.

Another event that shook the very foundations of Afrikaners and their theological self-justification was the discovery of diamonds and gold in South Africa. As a result, there was a huge influx of miners from throughout the world, who rushed to South Africa to try and make quick money. This had consequences for the Afrikaners, who prided themselves on being an agricultural people. According to Akenson:

> Thus, the discoveries of diamonds and gold had the paradoxical effect of making the Afrikaner states potentially economically more powerful, while at the same time threatening the character of their culture which was based on dispersed agricultural holdings, on common folk memories of historical events, and on similar, but loosely defined, attitudes towards the land and to religion. Within this context, the hordes of miners were as much a cultural threat as an economic one.[14]

Inevitably, the discovery of this kind of economic strength along with the increasing independence of the Afrikaners in various inland states (Transvaal Republic and the Republic of the Orange Free State) led to conflict. Alongside a series of Anglo-Boer wars, as they became known, there was an increase in organization by people who were designated black or coloured. In 1902, 'Coloureds in Capetown' formed the African People's Organization. This group was set up in order to address increasing (and long-standing) oppression of the African people by Afrikaner colonizers and descendants of colonizers.

By 1909, the British were ready to let go of some control of South Africa, and they decided to try and unify the different states that were established in South Africa under one banner. The South Africa Act of 1909 brought into one union the four regions of the Cape Colony, the Natal, the Transvaal and the Orange Free State. Initially the union was under the British empire and its rules. However, this relationship would eventually be dissolved because of these British rules and regulations, especially on issues related to social justice and race. Advocacy groups for indigenous South Africans continued to try and influence the newly formed union, especially via the British empire. This was especially in relation to ownership of land, fair treatment under the law, and workplace legislations. Their pleas were to no avail, however, and as the British influence moved away from South Africa, the rules against indigenous South Africans – and indeed any person of colour – became increasingly harsh. This is the precursor to the system that became known as apartheid. And yes, this system was also theologically justified.

The word 'apartheid' first appeared in South African vernacular in the 1940s. What should be noted, however, is that the practice of apartheid was something that had been developing for a long time. Many of the theologies we will discuss that are considered 'bad' theology were not theological ideas that appeared out of nowhere. They were slowly integrated into the fabric of society in a way that most people would not notice. This is an incredibly dangerous form of bad theology because people do not notice that they are already in the system until it is too late.

As the British moved their control away from South Africa, the Afrikaners saw an opportunity to fulfil what they believed to be their divine destiny when it came to the land they inhabited. What was needed for this new era of Afrikaner rule in South Africa was nationalism. They needed to clarify what had often been a rather diverse notion of what it meant to be an Afrikaner. When looking to what could create a more unifying vision of Afrikaner identity in South Africa, many leaders looked to the church (and specifically theology) to create an identity and a mission for Afrikaners. Dr D. F. Malan (a former minister who would be Prime Minister of South Africa in 1948) is quoted as saying:

> Our [Afrikaner] history is the greatest masterpiece of the centuries. We hold this nationhood as our due for it was given to us by the Architect of the universe. [His] aim was the formation of a new nation among the nations of the world … the last hundred years have witnessed a miracle behind which lies a divine plan. Indeed the history of the Afrikaner reveals a will and a determination which makes one feel that Afrikanerdom is the work of men but the creation of God.[15]

The unified vision for the Afrikaners was this idea of the covenantal and providential relationship that they had with God. They created a community out of a shared history that placed them as the children of Israel, just in a different landscape. From the imperialism of the British and the consequent wars of independence, they saw a divine plan in motion. This plan meant that God was with them throughout their struggles. The Great Trek was thus an exodus event that saw them try to find a new land for their people. The victory over the Zulu at Blood River was seen as being like the victory of the Israelites over the Philistines. It was at this victory that a covenant was established and oaths were taken. The covenantal relationship led them into the promised land, which were their own territories of Transvaal and the Orange Free State. The defeat by the British in 1902 was seen as God testing his chosen people in order to show them why they needed to be in covenant with God. All that to say, 'Their struggle was not over. They still had that eschatological vision which anticipated once again the rebirth of a republic in which Afrikaner would be the free and undisputed ruler under the providence of the Almighty.'[16] In one of those slow-developing bad theology viewpoints, there was an increasingly racist theology that was moving alongside the need to be rulers of their own land. Because of the idea that the Afrikaners were the covenantal people of God there was a need to know how to interact with people who were not a part of that covenant, according to the Afrikaner's theology. The answer for Afrikaners as to how to deal with outsiders was a theological idea they called 'separate development', which of course would later be known as apartheid.

Separate development began as a theological idea that God had created different races purposefully, and that each race was placed in a given geographical area and had specific missions and intentions. For this Afrikanerdom to grow and prosper under God, there was a need to maintain the essential nature of what it means to be an Afrikaner. Afrikaners had a specific reason to be on the planet, and they had to maintain that identity in order to fulfil their covenantal agreement with God. There was a time when the British synods in South Africa were able to temper this belief with their own theological counterarguments, but as Britain withdrew from South Africa, so did these voices – or at least the power of the voices in making laws.

This reality was about to take a firm hold with the general election of 1948. According to Akenson:

> The one major way in which the Afrikaner people of the early 20th century differed from their ancient Hebrew models was that they did not have the power to make laws themselves. The Afrikaner's covenantal cultural grid implied a great deal of concern with the sacred and the profane and with right and wrong behavior ... a covenantal society requires more than voluntary discipline, however.[17]

The general election of 1948 would give life to this dream for the Afrikaners. Their party, the Nationalists, won an absolute parliamentary majority. The Afrikaners had mobilized the white vote in South Africa, and they had done so by using a theological understanding of the nation, with a particular emphasis on separate development; this proved very attractive to the white population.

Widely held beliefs of Afrikaners at this time were that God had created divinely separate orders of people in the world. While other nations had seen a mixing of these orders, or races, the Afrikaners had created a pure society that was operating under what was the ultimate will of God for humanity:

> The South African state was put on earth to preserve intact a line of divinely ordered historical development, a line that ran from the creation to the end of human history. This belief, along with the belief that Afrikaner culture was one of the purist bastions of western civilization, was widely held by the Afrikaner population.[18]

There was a battle going on between what were seen as superior civilizations and those civilizations that had weakened themselves through intermixing with other civilizations; Afrikaners saw this as being against God's intention for humanity: 'Western civilization has destroyed itself in titanic struggle ... and with it the Divinely ordained divisions between East and West and between the white men and the coloured races.'[19]

Increasing power in the legislative areas of South African life led to the inevitable reality of a Prime Minister who was a firm believer in this type of bad theology. D. F. Malan was elected Prime Minister of South Africa in 1948, and advocated the bad theology that has been mentioned here; and also theology that continued to develop among Dutch Reformed clergy who felt emboldened by their newly established political power. The theological idea of 'trusteeship' became increasingly popular. What this trusteeship meant was that God had ordained that white men would act as trustees over the rest of the population because 'trusteeship was necessary because the blacks were like children. And there was a spiritual trust involved.'[20] This theme of trusteeship was seen in Afrikaner theology in the 1950s and 1960s.

The theology of trusteeship continued to develop as the Afrikaners gained more political power. In 1953, the Federal Missionary Council of the Dutch Reformed Churches met together in Pretoria to discuss the future of their society in relation to people from different races and backgrounds. They confirmed that what they described as 'natural diversity' was actually a system ordained by God; in other words, God created separate nations and different races on the earth for a reason, and each group had its own providential purpose. The group adopted theological reasoning when it came to religiously justifying apartheid in practice. The first of these reasonings was that the Dutch Reformed churches had always taken mission to non-Europeans very seriously. So seriously, in fact, that they had learned their languages in order to express the Christian message in a way that non-Europeans would understand linguistically. The NGK synod agreed that this was a 'natural separation'; and affirmed and that while it was desirable for all Christians to worship together, there would occasionally be instances of 'weakness' in a person or a group that meant they had to worship separately.

Following these decisions there were a series of Acts passed that codified apartheid into the law of the land. Again, all of these Acts were justified by the history and theology of the Afrikaners in South Africa. The Prohibition of Mixed Marriages Act of 1949 banned marriages between people considered whites and non-whites. This was seen as directly related to the covenantal culture of keeping oneself pure and so maintaining the European view on Christian trusteeship of non-whites in the country. A further Act in 1950 prohibited sexual relations between whites and non-whites for the same reason. A Jim Crow-esque law called the Reservation of Separate Amenities Act of 1953 further separated people in South Africa by allowing public spaces to be racially controlled and divided. This included buses, libraries, parks, trains, water fountains, toilets, bars, restaurants and so on.[21] These separate spaces had no

regulation of being equal opportunities for all people. Similarly, jobs and education were all segregated and the inequality
that resulted from this specifically hit the indigenous South
Africans and non-whites.

In 1948, the Institute for Christian Education, which regulated
the separation of the races in education, published a report
that had the following theological justification for its actions:

> We believe that every nation is rooted in its own soil which
> is allotted to it by the Creator. Every citizen of our country
> must have sound knowledge of our land ... and this know-
> ledge must be communicated in such a way that the pupil
> will love their own soil, also in comparison and contrast with
> other countries ... We believe that history must be taught
> in the light of the divine revelation and must be seen as the
> fulfillment of God's decree for the world and humanity ...
> We believe that God has willed separate nations and peoples,
> and has given each separate nation and peoples its particular
> vocation and tasks and gifts ... We believe that next to the
> mother-tongue, the patriotic history of the nation is the great
> means of cultivating love of one's own.[22]

According to Akenson, these Acts were all part of something
historians call 'petty apartheid'. That being said, Acts that
related to 'grand apartheid' were also in place. The Group
Area Acts of 1950 separated territories by race; and not only
territories – cities were also sectioned off for people of different races to reside. In 1966, the General Synod of NGK
confirmed this belief in a document called *Human Relations
in South Africa*. Within the document were previously articulated theological ideas that confirmed a belief in apartheid for
Afrikaners: 'Ethnic diversity is in agreement with God's will.'[23]
Akenson goes on to summarize that the document confirmed:
'[blurring] by racial mixing the distinctiveness and character of
various groups was sinful'.[24]

At this stage the international community was starting to
take notice of the actions in South Africa; but these attacks

from outside, of course, would also be theologically answerable by the Afrikaners in South Africa. According to the covenantal culture, the belief was that there is always going to be an attack on the Afrikaners, much like the Israelites. There should never be compromise with these attacks, however, and the attacks on the righteous by the unrighteous showcased the connection the Afrikaner community had with God. In a study conducted by J. M. du Preez, further information was uncovered about the Afrikaner mindset that was being passed down to children in segregated schools. This information was as follows: one does not question authority; whites are superior to non-whites; Afrikaners have an exclusive relationship with God; Afrikaners are farmers as well as a military powerhouse; Afrikaners are isolated; Afrikaners are constantly being threatened by non-Afrikaner populations and cultures; South Africa is a leader in the continent of Africa; and Afrikaners have a God-given mission for the land of South Africa. Du Preez concludes that the national theology is summarized (and passed down) as follows:

> The Afrikaner identifies with the Jewish people of the Old Testament. The History textbooks and Afrikaans setworks in particular are written in the idiom of the Old Testament, e.g. the mission of the chosen people; the epic journey through the desert, all sorts of trials and tribulations; the heathens who are exterminated, the preservation of a pure White nation; the Covenant that binds the people to God; judges (national leaders) and other symbols or master symbols.[25]

While we could continue with this history, I am stopping here to take a snapshot of this specific theological community during a certain timeline; and I will be doing this with all four case studies. Although one could write volumes on the entire history of a place and a time and a people, I want to dive deeper into this particular snapshot: the Afrikaner theological development, or lack thereof, as Afrikaners first arrive in South Africa and their subsequent ascendency into power. Some ideas developed, others remained firmly in place, but the bad theology here is clear.

A bad theology of providence

> Afrikaner politics was slowly but fatally being theologized. There was a growing urge to set the South African world aright, once and for all, to reconstruct it and redeem it in terms of a newly-defined Afrikaner *lewens-en-wereldbeskouing* – a world view.[26]

Providence, as was discussed briefly at the beginning of this chapter, has to do with the way in which God does or does not work in the world for those who follow God. This idea has been discussed in all of the monotheistic traditions, and Christianity was no exception. What is particular to the South African Afrikaner theology is that it bases its understanding of providence on the Old Testament view of the covenants of God, not on the New Testament. In fact, the New Testament is almost completely avoided by Afrikaner theology in this snapshot. This makes sense, bearing in mind some of the themes that emerge from the New Testament, including equality and justice. 'Yet, on the other hand, they had to deal with Christianity's doctrine of the equality of all persons before the Almighty. Much ingenious theology was the result, of the sort that reminds one of the suggestion that the real purpose of most theology is to make excuses for the behavior of both God and man.'[27]

The Old Testament themes that do come out of this snapshot all relate to God's providence and God's covenant with the Afrikaner people. If we examine their theology in relation to the criteria for bad theology, we can see that this snapshot of theology of the Afrikaner people fits within each category.

Under criterion 1, your theology is used to limit human flourishing. This one is quite easy based on the conversation at hand. The Afrikaner people felt from the beginning that they

were fighting against everyone in South Africa (divinely fighting it should be added). They were God's people, and God was
providentially working for them in this context for their ultimate ascension to ruling the land that was set aside for them.
The problem with this theological idea is that there were other
indigenous people on the land, as well as other colonists fighting for power in the same context. Even before their move into
politics, Afrikaner theology focused on the promotion of the
Afrikaner people over and against any other member of the
population. The Afrikaners were the Israelites and everyone
who was not a part of their group were considered Canaanite,
who were those trying to prevent the completion of God's will
in South Africa.

Eventually, this would lead to the concept of separate development that limited human flourishing to an extreme level. In
an attempt to live out their notion of God's preference of their
particular cultural group, they had to limit interactions with
other groups in order to remain pure and sinless. This limiting ultimately led to legislation that unequally separated those
who were from different backgrounds from the Afrikaner and
led to the system of apartheid that influenced everything –
geography, education, jobs and human interaction generally.
This separation would negatively affect human flourishing,
and it was at the core of the theology of the Afrikaners in this
snapshot.

Theologically, the Afrikaners used the story of the Israelites
in order to avoid criterion 2. A lack of self-reflection was a given
in the community, and anyone who challenged the status quo
was not challenging the government or even the church; therefore those who challenged were challenging God's providence.
A respect of authority was taught in the schools. The history
and theology of the community was accepted as fact, and those
who went against this history and theology were considered
outsiders, ungodly and communists! This created an atmosphere of self-justification as well as fear of challenging those
who created the narrative for the community. This was not an
atmosphere that welcomed any self-reflection outside of the

created story that existed and was accepted as true. And this lack of challenge was passed on through the generations within the context of Afrikaner school system.

An us versus them mentality that is the key to understanding criterion 3 is right at the core of the covenantal understanding that Afrikaners had in this snapshot. The very nature of God's providence and the covenant that the Afrikaners had with God puts their community at the centre of the story of South Africa. From the beginning there is an idea that mixing (culturally, physically, legally) was a sin against God's plan for the community. This mentality led to the separate development idea that would eventually lead to the system of apartheid in South Africa. Afrikaners believed that God ordained them to remain separate from other cultures in South Africa – white or indigenous South Africans, it did not matter. Either way, the Afrikaners were to keep themselves distinct in the midst of a multicultural world. Criterion 3 also states that there is no desire within your theology to interact with those outside your community. While the emotion 'desire' is hard to interpret, what we can see from the Afrikaner educational system, as well as the Acts passed that related to separate development, meant that there was no real interaction between Afrikaners and other communities within South Africa. So the idea that there would be a desire to interact may be ambitious. There was just no opportunity to interact – desire or not. By keeping Afrikaners separate from other races from birth to death in most aspects of everyday life, they eliminated the need to enforce separation. By taking away all the opportunities to interact with people who are different, they also took away any notions one might have even to attempt such an interaction.

This leads almost directly into criterion 4, which relates to the fact that your theology leads you to believe that you should isolate yourselves from the rest of the world. A follow-up to criterion 4 is the understanding that you most likely had little choice in your theology or belief system. This concept is seen clearly in the Afrikaner mindset of separation. They have their very own exodus story, the Trek, that highlights to their community the lengths they would go in order to follow God's plan for their lives. By leaving the oppression of the British at the Cape colonies, the Afrikaners were escaping persecution in order to fully realize God's plan for them. Upon reaching Blood Creek, and eventually defeating the Zulu, they had overcome their obstacles in order to set up a new society. They committed that community to God in a covenant. This story of the exodus of the Afrikaners highlights how they wanted to find a place where they could exercise their version of Christianity outside the constraints of British laws. Also, based on the studies into Afrikaner education and their strict internal rules about remaining pure, it is clear that those inside the community had little to no choice in relation to what they were taught. While internally they might question, externally they were expected to toe the party line, or be exiled as a usurper.

Afrikaners had a very particular view on the way that their theology operated in the wider world. Social justice or political change didn't matter much to their theological views (unless the political change helped their own cause). This was because they held the theological view that God was providential and was in charge of what was happening in the world. The Afrikaners' actions in the world were according to the will of God, and God's covenant with them. As a result, the need to intervene in worldly things seemed of little importance to the Afrikaners.

The search for justice, criterion 5, would have been seen as being of little importance to the community. With such a high theology of God's providence, it would be almost insulting to think that their actions in the world would change anything outside of God's will. As a result, they remained isolated and unconcerned with things of the world, including justice. One area of mission that they did see as important was that of converting people to the Christian tradition, but even that was to be done separately, whereby each community was in charge of their own souls.

Criterion 6, the need for equality in the wider world, is a really good conclusion to this particular section. In this snapshot of the world of the Afrikaners, equality does not exist; the opposite is prevalent throughout their theology. Instead of everyone in the world being equal, there is a key belief that Afrikaners are separate and special. They are not equal to other people in their country. They are a covenantal group who has been chosen by God. God is working towards the good of their particular community. So much so, in fact, that Afrikaners do not need to mix with other communities in order to maintain this pure superiority. The reason that separate development was able to exist was because of this theological understanding of the cultural, racial and communal superiority of the Afrikaners in relation to others in the wider world. As a result, Afrikaners theologically justified an unequal system, not just a separate system. There was no clause in their Acts to make anything equal in the law under apartheid. This is because the desire to maintain purity in terms of their own special status far outweighs the needs of those who were not inside the covenant. God would do with other people as God chose. That was not up to the Afrikaners, that was up to God, and as a result they did not bother themselves with the details of the situations of those who were being continually oppressed by the apartheid system. By turning a blind eye, in their view they were letting God be God in the world. It was God's will who was chosen and who was not. And those who were not were left to fend for themselves in an unequal and unjust system.

Notes

1 Charles Wood, 'Providence' in *The Oxford Handbook of Systematic Theology*, ed. John Webster, Kathryn Tanner and Iain Torrance (Oxford: Oxford University Press, 2007), pp. 91–2.

2 David Fergusson, 'The Theology of Providence', *Theology Today* 67.3 (2010), pp. 261–78.

3 Fergusson, 'The Theology of Providence', p. 265.

4 Fergusson, 'The Theology of Providence', p. 267.

5 Fergusson, 'The Theology of Providence', p. 267.

6 Donald Harman Akenson, *God's People* (Montreal: McGill-Queen's University Press, 1992), p. 206.

7 Language around whites, non-whites, coloured, black, indigenous and so on are all language choices that get thrown around a great deal in the histories of South Africa. For the purposes of this book, I try and adopt a clearer language that relates to where people originated or self-identify as opposed to skin colour, which can vary even among people from similar parts of the world. One designation that I will be making is that of Afrikaners and South Africans. Afrikaners are those who historically have Dutch origins and speak Afrikaans as a common language (along with their descendants). My distinction is to differentiate them from indigenous South Africans who originated in South Africa prior to colonists (and their descendants) arriving.

8 John W. de Gruchy, *The Church Struggle in South Africa* (London: SCM Press, 2004), pp. 1–2.

9 De Gruchy, *The Church Struggle in South Africa*, p. 2.

10 Akenson, *God's People*, p. 60.

11 Akenson, *God's People*, p. 61.

12 Akenson, *God's People*, p. 63.

13 De Gruchy, *The Church Struggle in South Africa*, p. 20.

14 Akenson, *God's People*, p. 65.

15 Malan in de Gruchy, *The Church Struggle in South Africa*, p. 30.

16 De Gruchy, *The Church Struggle in South Africa*, p. 30.

17 Akenson, *God's People*, p. 204.

18 Akenson, *God's People*, p. 205.

19 Quoted from *Die Volksblad* in Akenson, *God's People*, p. 205.

20 Akenson, *God's People*, p. 206.

21 Akenson, *God's People*, p. 211.

22 Institute of Christian National Education quoted in Akenson, *God's People*, pp. 217–18.

23 *Human Relations in South Africa* quoted in Akenson, *God's People*, p. 207.

24 Akenson, *God's People*, p. 207.

25 Du Preez quoted in Akenson, *God's People*, p. 223.

26 W. A. de Klerk in de Gruchy, *The Church Struggle in South Africa*, p. 33.

27 Akenson, *God's People*, p. 206.

5

John Winthrop and John Mason: A Bad Theology of Election

Election and theology

The idea of God's election can be traced back to some of the earliest theological developments in the church. The doctrine of election is tied very closely to that of predestination, which sees God as having control over the trajectory of God's created world. Election takes this notion a step farther and says that God also has control over God's believers and followers and desires them to reach communion with God. In the Old Testament we see election almost immediately through the children of Israel, the Jewish people, who God says are God's chosen people. The language is very explicit in acknowledging that the Israelites are God's special community, and consequently that God will take care of them. This care is enacted through a variety of leaders who speak directly with God and look out for the community, and also through the range of covenants (promises) that God makes between Godself and the Israelites. While the stories of the Israelites as God's chosen people, or the elect, are prevalent throughout the Old Testament, we see them predominantly in the books Deuteronomy and Isaiah. The reasoning behind this chosenness is debated in different groups within Judaism, but the focus appears to be on the idea of the Israelites and consequent generations embodying the greatness of God in the world.

From the New Testament, Augustine advocated the idea that salvation was a grace given freely by God – albeit undeserved by humans because of the sin that permeates their lives. The philosopher Pelagius argued against the notion of original sin put forth by Augustine, in which he did not believe because he regarded it as unfair that some people would be blamed for other people's sins. Pelagius even went so far as to say it was possible to live a sinless life if one did not choose to disobey the laws of God. While Augustine had a very high view of God and a lower view of humanity (in terms of sin), Pelagius had a high view of humanity. He saw humans as being creations of God and therefore capable of having a conscience, and making decisions on their own about how they will live their lives. Humans, as a result, were to be held responsible for their own actions, including that of choosing or not choosing God, according to Pelagius. Augustine advocated that any positive actions that people did in the world should be attributed to the elect nature that God had bestowed on creation. Accordingly, and sometimes controversially, he said that because grace was a gift from God (not a reward), certain people were elected to receive it and others were not. Humans were diseased with sin, according to Augustine, and they needed God's grace in order to be free from this sinful state. In summary, in Augustine's world all praise and credit for any positivity in the world was due to God alone, not human endeavours.[1]

After the Pelagian controversies, the next two big theological debates that we see in terms of the theology of election come via John Calvin and Jacobus (Jacob) Arminius. Calvin was convinced that the theology of election meant that God has determined that certain people will reach salvation, and that this is all part of God's sovereignty over creation. He believed that predestination as a theological concept was to help people understand the difficult idea that God chooses some of them to reach salvation and others not to reach it. Predestination is not something that Calvin focuses exclusively on in terms of theology, nor is it something he spends a great deal of time on (despite Calvinists who believe otherwise). He discussed the idea that if people go to heaven, or if they are condemned to hell (double predestination), they are ultimately operating within the will of God; this line of thought was not something to be challenged or debated.[2] According to Calvin, humans are born as enemies of God, and as a result any grace that God extends towards humanity is mercy on God's part.

Jacob Arminius had a very different take on the ideas around election and predestination. He rejected the reformed view of predestination and believed instead that Jesus had died for the entirety of humanity, not just the elect. This idea was considered and debated, especially within evangelical denominations. John Wesley, the founder of the Methodists, was a strong advocate of what became known as Arminianism.[3]

The Swiss theologian Karl Barth famously discoursed around election and predestination. Needless to say, for scholars of Barth, his entire understanding of election lies in the life and death of Jesus Christ. Barth believed that people have free will, and he also acknowledged that God was aware that not everyone would reach awareness of God. Before the beginning of creation, God decided that Jesus was elected to be the great reconciler for humanity. God, as a result, does not choose those who are to be elect and reach salvation, but instead Jesus stands as the ultimate election umbrella. Humans are reconciled to God through the choice of Jesus as the substitute for the election. If humans accept Jesus' reconciliation then they also get added to his election status, according to Barth. The life of Jesus and his eventual death on the cross occur so that the judgement of God is not placed upon the backs of the human race.[4]

Alongside Barth, many theologians continue to debate and discuss the doctrine of election. It is a tough pill to swallow for some: the idea that God would choose (whether before creation or after) to save some from eternal damnation and not others. Some theologians, especially in the reformed tradition, claim that there is nothing that can be done about this because the scriptures seem to indicate that there is something that must be said about God's grace in relation to humanity. Other theologians argue that the idea that God chooses some and not others says a lot about a judgmental God and not a lot about grace. Inevitably, this debate will continue, and as we move towards the snapshot for this chapter it is important to realize that the Puritans who came to the colonies had a very strong understanding of the reformed view of election. It is important because this theology will underpin many of the decisions that will lead people down the path of bad theology.

John Winthrop and the 'New World'

While there were many different colonial journeys to the 'New World', the focus of this section will be specifically on England's first Puritan colonies in North America. The Puritans were not the only pocket of religion that existed in the early days of the colonies. The Spanish and French had settlements in the south-west; the Virginia colonies had other Christian groups; the Quakers lived in Pennsylvania; Catholics had taken up residency in Maryland; and African traditional religions came to the Americas via the slave trade. In addition, there were the indigenous people who were already practising their religion when the colonists arrived. All these showcased the religious diversity of the New World.[5]

That being said, some scholars argue for the primacy of the Puritan communities with regard to influence at the beginning of the new country. According to Walter Herbert, who is referencing Perry Miller, 'The origins of the American self, as it is commonly taught, are to be found among the English Puritans on the Atlantic seaboard.'[6] This idea is debatable considering the sheer number of people who were in the colonies at the time. Accordingly, it seems difficult to pinpoint one colonial group as being the heart and soul of the USA. What we can say is that the Puritans *believed* themselves to be this heart and soul, and their presence was hugely influential in the grand scheme of the colonialization of the USA. From their voyage from England, their theological beliefs are at the centre of their actions as colonists. According to Herbert:

The Massachusetts Bay Puritans conceived themselves as God's chosen – Christian inheritors of God's covenant with Abraham – and visualized the place of their new world settlement as the 'promised land'. Just as ancient Israel was liberated by God from Egyptian bondage, taken into a covenant at Mount Sinai, and led through the desert to their appointed land, so the Puritans had escaped Anglican piety under a Catholic monarch, had passed through the wilderness of waters, and now sought to live out the covenant in the land God had prepared for them.[7]

The story of the Puritans in the USA begins with the story of religion in Europe. Within Europe, state-sponsored churches were the norm in many countries. The reasoning behind these types of churches was to show a united front with regard to religion. This move was largely political, the assumption being a united religion would lead to a united (and strong) population. The national churches were almost completely determined by the leaders of European countries at a given time. With Henry VIII in power, England became a Protestant nation, with all people within the country moving to the newly separated Church of England. Though the country would switch back to Roman Catholicism under Mary I, ultimately the Church of England would regain the monarch's approval under Elizabeth I, who was strict in her allegiance to it and expected her citizens to be likewise. She did take on board calls for reform in the Church, however, and continued to eliminate practices that appeared too Catholic. Elizabeth I was not understanding of groups that she saw as splinter Protestant communities. Again, this was less about ideology or theology and more about having a united religious front in England. In the 1580s, she banned meetings for Protestants that she considered to be radical, or 'schismatics', or those Protestants who wanted to separate from the Church of England.[8]

Under Elizabeth's successor, James I (of England), Protestant groups demanding further reforms from the Church of England multiplied. These groups became known as 'Puritans' because of the view that their protests represented a form of religious zealousness. The Puritans saw themselves in a battle with Roman Catholics (both in terms of power and theology). They did not appreciate what they saw as the adoption of Reformation ideals into the Roman Catholic Church structure. They held firmly to ideas adopted by the Protestant church during the Reformation. James I tried to suppress the Puritans and their calls for reform, but by the 1630s they had become too numerous to silence. While some Puritan groups (and other 'dissenting' Protestant groups) worked with the Church of England in order to continue reform, still others decided to begin anew in the New World.

It was these Puritans who first came to the USA in the 1600s and established colonies in Massachusetts. The original Puritan colonists landed near Plymouth, Massachusetts, where they set up their first settlement. By 1630, there was continued oppression of Puritans in England, and as a result larger numbers of colonists began to move to the Massachusetts Bay colony. The Puritans saw the move as a means of showcasing to the world a truly biblical model of Christian community. This larger group of Puritans was led by the lawyer John Winthrop, whose Calvinist theology became the central ideology of this group of colonists. Winthrop was a man of wealth and education in England but, with the increasing pressures of the King, as well as economic difficulties as a result of his Puritan faith, he decided to join fellow Puritans heading to the colonies.

The Massachusetts Bay Puritans decided that Winthrop should be governor of their new colony because of his education and background. As a result of this new status, Winthrop articulated a vision for the future of the Puritan colony via a sermon called 'A Model of Christian Charity'. This vision would be the framework into which the Puritans would arrange their beliefs, their society and, most importantly, their actions in the New World. The language that was used in Winthrop's speech relies heavily on theological ideas related to covenant, election and prosperity.[9] These three theological ideas are common in conversations related to bad Practical Theology. Though not 'bad' theological conclusions in themselves, we do see that these four areas are *easily manipulated* into means of colonialism and various iterations of oppression globally.

Winthrop begins his sermon/speech with a discussion of election. He states that, 'God Almighty, in his most holy and wise providence, hath so disposed of the condition of mankind, as in all times some must be rich, some poor, some high and eminent in power and dignity; others mean and in submission.'[10] The idea of God's providence being at the centre of the whole of Christian life remains a constant throughout the sermon, and indeed the Puritan theology generally speaking. God predetermines the way of the world, according to Winthrop, and not all are able to be of equal status. Accordingly, he writes, God is 'delighted to show forth the glory of his wisdom in the variety and difference of the creatures, and the glory of his power in ordering all these differences for the preservation and good of the whole'.[11] Winthrop did believe that God has preordained certain people to have a certain status according to God's will. This was all, according to Winthrop, a result of God's infinite understanding of the way of the world. These orders were what kept society together, and they would continue to exist in the new colonies.

Almost as a result of this ordering, Winthrop put forth a strong message concerning the importance of community. One commandment above them all was the key to 'moral law',[12] according to Winthrop. 'Love your neighbour as yourself' was the message that he repeats over and over in his sermons. It is clear in his writings that he believes that loving your neighbour as yourself is what will keep society together in a new land. A part of loving your neighbour as yourself is the sharing of wealth and assets across the community. In line with his belief that not all people are preordained to the same level of wealth and power, he does see that those who have more should give to those who have less. There are some caveats to this type of charity, however, in that charity should be extended especially to those who are a part of the same religious community as you. He states: 'Do good to all, especially to the household of faith; upon this ground the Israelites were to put a difference between the brethren of such as were strangers though not of the Canaanites.'[13] This likening of the Puritans to the children of Israel is present throughout much of Winthrop's sermon. It is quite obvious that the Puritans saw themselves as an elect people, going to a promised land from God, in order to live out their lives in a way that would serve as an example to the rest of the world.

One key aspect of comparing the Puritans to the children of Israel is that Winthrop adopted some of the stories of the Israelites into the story of the Puritans. One such story, which would become important later in the days of the colony, was that of Amalek. Much like the children of Israel, the Puritans believed that they were united in a covenant agreement with God. With this covenant, God would protect the Puritans, but only if the Puritans continued to observe and obey the laws of God. Accordingly, Winthrop references the Old Testament story of God's command to Saul to kill everyone in the nation of Amalek. According to the biblical narrative, the Amalekites were longstanding enemies of the Israelites. Saul is called by God to kill every living thing in Amalek, sparing no one (1 Samuel 15.2–3). But Saul does in fact spare someone, King Agag. As a result of this rebellion God punishes Saul, and he loses his own status as King (1 Samuel 15.23).

Saul's punishment, according to Winthrop, is a direct result of his betrayal of God's commands. Winthrop claims the same will happen to the Puritans if they do not also obey the agreement with God. The consequences of a betrayal of the covenant agreement with God will be severe. According to Winthrop: '[If we] shall fall to embrace this present world and prosecute our carnal intentions, seeking great things for ourselves and our posterity, the Lord will surely break out in wrath against us; be revenged of such a sinful people and make us know the price of the breach of such a covenant.'[14] Winthrop is quick to say, however, that the Puritans would be able to set up their own rules in the new colony, according to God's will, but that the people would be required to follow these rules strictly in order to keep God happy in the covenant.

Winthrop believed that the Puritans would set up their colony like a 'city of God' or a 'city upon a hill'.[15] He believed that the new colony would serve as an example to all those who were desirous of living in Christian community. Winthrop states: 'We shall find that the God of Israel is among us, when ten of us shall be able to resist a thousand of our enemies; when he shall make us a praise and glory that men shall say of succeeding plantations, "the Lord make it likely that of New England".'[16] This new England would be unlike the last England in many ways. The Puritans saw themselves as being on a covenantal mission with God. This mission meant that they would establish a true Christian community in accordance with the desires of God on earth. According to Herbert:

> Puritans intended that the exemplary community in New England, living strictly in accordance with biblical precepts, would provide an inspiration to the international effort and a model for others to follow. This would happen if, but only if, the community remained faithful to the ethical duties God had set forth to govern their life together.[17]

These ideas that were the foundation of Puritan life are not altogether new. The mirroring of the lives of the Israelites and the promises God made to them is a common theme in justifying occupying already occupied lands. It could be presumed that the Puritans might have existed with their belief systems firmly in place without a major theological issue for quite some time, self-justifying with little reflection. That being said, their covenant theology was ultimately a practical theology of colonial living. As a result, they soon were using their own theological understandings to attempt to realize their status as chosen people.

Almost immediately upon the arrival of the Puritans in the New World there was conflict. A critical area of surprise for the colonists was the fact that there were other people living in their promised land. The Puritans largely maintained their theology in relation to being a covenantal, chosen people who were to establish a city on a hill in the promised land, all under the supportive gaze of an omnipotent creator. Not all members of the colony were of one mind and body, however. Roger Williams served as a vocal opponent of many of the ideas that the leadership of the Massachusetts Bay colony put forward, especially in relation to the native peoples of the land they were currently occupying.

Williams challenged the Puritan leadership on two key points. First, he did not believe that the Puritans had a right to the land they were living on just because they thought it was the promised land. Williams questioned the transmission of the Israelite covenant to that of the Puritans. He did not see this as a physical covenantal link, but instead one that was a spiritual covenant only. As a result, he believed that the colonists did not have a right to forcibly remove the first people from their land based on theological reasonings. Second, Williams argued that colonists should be allowed to challenge the Puritan authority without fear of punishment. Needless to say, both of these claims were promptly rejected by the leadership of the colony. Those in charge needed to have the whole of the colony in one mind, and this one mind was based on the idea of the Puritans as the chosen people for those chosen lands. Any dissent from this conclusion undermined the very theology upon which the Puritans existed in Massachusetts Bay. Williams was promptly banished from the colony, and consequently set up his own community in Rhode Island. It should be noted that he purchased this land from the native Narragansetts who were living there at the time.

Why was it so important for Williams to be banished from his Puritan community? Surely, based on the words of Winthrop, one should extend the hand of peace to one's brother or sister of the faith? According to Miller, in Herbert's *Faith-Based War*: 'Williams was not merely a social nuisance, but a real danger to the very structure of Puritan society.'[18] As there was no true legal claim to the land that the colonists were occupying (other than being ceremoniously granted by a colonizing mother country), the colonists needed a justified status in their place in the New World. Williams, by threatening the very theology upon which this justified status sat, threatened the continuation of the entire colony. Accordingly, the need for this theological justification was so strong that any dissenting voices had to be removed. The consequences of people moving into theological factions was too great at this stage for the Puritans. They had to be of one unified, covenanted mind.

The Puritans existed for some time on the land they occupied by making treaties and alliances with native populations. The true test in diplomacy for the Puritans came by way of the Pequot tribe, who had long pushed back against the Puritans moving into their lands. While there was acknowledgement that the Pequot nation was on the land prior to the Puritans, there was little by way of respect for that primacy. As Anders Stephanson writes: 'For Europeans, land not occupied by recognized members of Christendom was theoretically land free to be taken.'[19] While the idea of the taking of land from the native populations was common among Europeans, it was only the Puritans who saw the land they occupied as being sacred. England was not a sacred territory because of its decisions that were against God's plan, according to the Puritans, but the New World was a sacred land for a sacred people. If this land is occupied by God's chosen people, it brings people closer to a true reconciliation (or salvation) with God. According to Stephanson: 'Through the New Israel, universal righteousness will return and the world will be regenerated.'[20] As a result, keeping the covenant was more than just a colonial situation for the Puritan colony; it was a mission from God for the soul of the country (and beyond).

The Puritans did not react positively to the Pequot and their desire to retain their own land. The Pequot had begun to mobilize among the tribes of New England. They had formed alliances with a variety of native groups, and as their numbers grew the Puritans became less comfortable in their position.

There had been violent interactions between the first people and the colonists, and the situation was escalating at a rapid rate. Ironically, the Puritans called upon the aid of Roger Williams, who – as we have seen – they had banished from their colony for dissent. Williams helped gain the Puritans an alliance with the Narragansetts and Mohegan tribes in order to combat the Pequot. However, this battle was more than just about square footage; it was about maintaining the promise they had made to God. According to Herbert: 'Were [the Puritans] to be expelled from the land that God had marked out for His covenant community? Or was their virtue sufficient to merit divine aid?'[21]

The 'aid' that the Puritans now looked towards was the leadership of one of their own, Captain John Mason, who prepared the colonists for the battle that was to come. Mason believed that the Pequot were a cruel people, who were violent and ill-willed to their very core. He stated that the Pequot were capable of 'outrageous violence' and that they created 'a quarrel against the English, who had never offered them the least wrong'.[22] The Puritans saw the native peoples as aggressors in their spiritual (and physical) journey in the new colony. The Pequot were not happy about their lands increasingly being occupied by foreigners who did not acknowledge their right to exist on them. There was also a struggle between the Pequot and other native groups in the region over control of trading between communities. The Pequot were gaining power and recognition for their superiority in trading tactics, and as a result the other tribes in the region felt threatened. Consequently, non-Pequot native communities began increasingly to align with the Puritan colonists. This was the set-up for the Pequot War that was to follow.

John Mason believed that the colonists would prevail in a battle against the Pequot. While there were battles here and there, the most disturbingly violent encounter between the two groups took place at the Pequot fort at Mystic River (Connecticut) in 1637. Backed by both the Mohegan and Narragansett tribes, the English colonists attacked the Pequot fort. As the colonists and allies attacked, the Pequot quickly mobilized in order to combat the incoming group. At the entrance of the fort, the Pequot managed to kill two of Mason's colonial men. Mason did not take this development well, and decided to burn down the entire settlement. He formed a circle around the fort, and the native allies formed a further circle around the English settlers. They set fire to the fort and shot anyone who tried to escape the burning. In the end, 400 members of the Pequot tribe were killed in this way, including women and children, who were not spared. Seven members of the tribe were captured and enslaved.

Mason describes the fight in detail in his account. He states that when the fire was started in the fort the flames 'swiftly [over-ran] the Fort, to the extreme amazement of the Enemy, and the great rejoicing of ourselves'.[23] Additionally, he wrote of the reaction of the Pequot to the fire: 'Thus were they now at their wits end, who not many hours before exalted themselves ... But God was above them, who laughed at his enemies and the enemies of his people to scorn, making them as a fiery oven.'[24] The linking between the violent actions of the settlers and their allies against the Pequot to a divine action was embraced by some colonials and rejected by others. Mason firmly believed that the actions that he was taking were God-commanded. Fellow Puritan William Bradford believed that the massacre at Mystic River was akin to the violence in the Old Testament. He linked the massacre in Connecticut to the battle of Amalek in the Old Testament (much like Winthrop before him used this imagery). He stated that the massacre was like that of the human sacrifice of Agag; a sacrifice that had to occur prior to God being satisfied with his command to Saul to kill all the Amalekites. Bradford offers the following: 'It was a fearful sight to see them thus frying in the fire ... and horrible was the stink and scent thereof; but the victory seemed a sweet sacrifice, and they [the English fighters] gave the praise therof to God.'[25]

Likewise, John Underhill, a Puritan leader in Massachusetts Bay, declared the battle to be completely under the direction

of God's purpose for the colonies. 'Yet Underhill insisted that
the biblical accounts of clearing the promised land offered sufficient justification. "I would refer you to David's war," he
declared.'[26] Underhill goes on to say that God does not have
respect for people who disobey God to the degree that the
Pequot had. Underhill adds: 'When a people is grown to such a
height of blood and sing against God ... he hath no respects for
persons, but harrows them and saws them, and puts them ... to
the most terriblest death that may be.'[27] Not only does Underhill theologically justify the way that the colonists viewed the
first people they massacred, but he also offers a plea of innocence for the way that the fighters undertook the destruction
at Mystic River. Again, directly referencing the Old Testament
story of Amalek, he says: 'Sometimes the Scripture declareth
that women and children must perish with their parents ...
We had sufficient light from the word of God for our proceed-
ings.'[28]

Not everyone was convinced by this particular theological
interpretation of what had happened to the Pequot. For the
exiled Roger Williams, this did not represent a Christian theology that he recognized. He believed that the Puritans had
fallen into the very sinful trap that Winthrop had warned them
about with regard to financial gains. The land that the colonists were wanting to expand into was valuable. There was a
direct association with this expansion to the continued economic growth of the settlers themselves. As a result, Williams
offers this rebuke to his fellow Puritans:

However you satisfy yourselves with the Pequot conquest,
yet upon a due and serious examination of the matter, in
the sight of God, you will find the business at bottom to be
... a depraved appetite after the great vanities, dreams and
shadows of this vanishing life ... This is one of the gods of
New England, which the living and most high Eternal will
destroy and famish.[29]

Williams did not view the success of the Puritans in the war against the Pequot as an indication of God's pleasure. He rejected the linking of the story of the Pequot to that of the Amalekites, and stated instead that the Puritans had lost their way with regard to their pursuit of money, power and land. Williams was not a pacifist, and he knew that sometimes armed conflict would be necessary. What he did not agree with was the adopted idea that any enemies of the self-proclaimed chosen people should be destroyed; or that any victory that these people might have over their enemies was God-ordained because God's people had made themselves worthy of such a victory. This understanding of 'divinely authorized war making'[30] did not sit well with Williams. According to Herbert:

> In the Massachusetts Bay ... the city serves as a bastion for those showing their Chosenness by conforming their minds and consciences to the edicts of the religious authorities. In exchange for relinquishing their moral autonomy they are given freedom to expand their wealth at the expense of the not-Chosen.[31]

Winthrop continued his leadership position in the Massachusetts Bay colony. In 1638, a local woman was accused by Winthrop of using witchcraft. His recordings of the midwife under suspicion (Jane Hawkins) was the first accusation in New England of witchcraft. In 1649, John Winthrop died; and the Puritan community that he had established looked very different at the end of his life from that which he had envisaged while on the flagship *Arbella* that took them to the colonies. According to Butler, Wacker and Balmer, much has been written about the Puritans during this period, but the reality of the state of the Puritans at the time of Winthrop's death is not as religious as some might believe. Some historians estimate that only 10–20 per cent of the total population actually belonged to a church during the colonial period.[32] Two churches were funded by the state at this time: the Congregationalists and the Episcopalians. However, as time marched on towards the

American Revolution, one finds that the active religious adherence of the general population was quite low. And while this adherence would not pick up until the revivalist movements, the theological ideas of those who were the first colonists in America pervaded society. The theological conclusions that were set by Winthrop and the first Puritan colonists were ideas that would come to define American identity throughout the years. 'Manifest Destiny' is another example of a bad theology that comes from this idea of the promised land and chosenness. That is bad theology for another day.

A bad theology of election

> Perhaps we might say that doctrines of God and God's acts cannot be fully reconciled without appeal – at least as a first step – to a doctrine of human knowledge of and language about God.[33]

The Puritans under Winthrop and the Battle of the Pequots under Mason are snapshots of the way that the theology of election was used as a means of divinely justifying extreme injustice and violence against indigenous people. This becomes clearer as we look at the sermons preached to the Puritans as they came to the colonies, as well as the reactions to the murders at Mystic River. If we examine the criteria for bad theology, we can see that the Puritans (within these two snapshots) fit the description of a bad theology of election.

Criterion 1 discusses the limiting of the flourishing of humans. While the Puritans felt as though they were embracing their status as God's chosen people in the New World, they were simultaneously limiting the flourishing of the indigenous people who were already living in colonial lands. Colonialization has used theology in multiple contexts to justify itself. In this case, the leadership preached the message that the Puritans were the elect. They believed they were chosen children of God (like the Israelites in the Old Testament). This status of election meant that they were in covenant with God, and they were to follow God's orders at all costs. God's orders were given to the community via the leadership in the community, and this leadership passed on this information to the rest of the Puritan group.

According to the leadership, God promised the Puritans the land of the colonies for the purpose of creating a city on a hill that would inspire everyone around them. Unfortunately, this entire theological plan was based firmly on the flourishing of the Puritans, and not of those who were already living on the land. The land of the native peoples was taken from them with no regard for payment or compensation or coexisting. When someone (Roger Williams) mentions the idea of compensating the native peoples, he is banished from the colony. Why, according to the Puritans, should we have to pay for lands that God has given us? Further, we see the complete disregard for human life in the battle at Mystic River. Men, women and children were burned alive while the Puritan leadership barely acknowledges these events. When they were acknowledged, they were seen as being akin to biblical stories of destruction. Sometimes women and children have to die, according to the leadership, in order for God to carry through God's plan. The descriptions of the sights, sounds and smells of this event showcase just how little the leadership cares about human flourishing. It also shows how little regard they had for those they considered outside their elect status.

Criterion 2 says that there is no self-reflection in your theology, and this is very clear in the examples of the Puritans in the early days of the colonies. While clearly there is very little reflection in the majority of bad theology, the examples that come from colonialization are often astounding. The Puritans were fed a line of theology that saw them as recreating the story of the Israelites as they are led out of Egypt into a promised land given to them by God. Along the way, God offers covenants to keep the Israelites close to God; the Puritans saw this as their story. They supposedly escaped the oppression in England and fled to the promised land that God had given them. In this land they would meet obstacles along the way, but the Puritans claimed justification for that as well. They likened their battles with the native peoples to those recounted in the Old Testament. God's people were occasionally called to divine violence in the Old Testament text, and the Puritans saw themselves as the elect who were also called to this kind of violence. The whole promised-land colonial story is not new, but it reflects the idea that once this narrative is presented to a people who are desperate for a new life, it sticks. It is very difficult at this stage to have any kind of reflection. And if reflection does exist it is seen as dissent against God and God's plan. Roger Williams attempted to call his community to reflect on their actions against the native peoples, and he was immediately banished from the community.

Based on previous paragraphs it is quite clear that criterion 3 is a key aspect of the bad theology of the Puritans. The election of the Puritans into the status of the chosen people means that they are divinely chosen to reside outside the realm of the rest of the world's population. It is not a case of choosing to be in community with those around them – they have been set aside as a chosen people, purposefully ordained to be in community. Essentially, the us versus them mentality is election. There are some people who are in, and there are some people who are out. The theological reasoning behind that in/out status is based on the notions of the theologians at hand, but ultimately there is an idea that some people are outside the covenant with God. There is not much manipulation of the theology that needs to take place here in order to have the Puritans desiring to interact only with their own community. There are no direct consequences of hanging around people who are not elect, according to the leaders, but it does seem like there is a 'What is the point?' mentality when it comes to these interactions. If those outside the elect community are seen as less than, which appears to be the case based on the reaction of the leadership to their violent deaths, then why mingle with those outside of God's preference? The Puritans were inherently isolationists, and they were quite keen to kick out anyone they deemed as not upholding their chosen status within the community. The us versus them mentality was a built-in, theological mechanism.

The Puritans were in a community, but they left everything they knew when they boarded the ships to go to the colonies. There is a reason why the Puritan community is featured in so many horror films, and it is only partly because of their theological beliefs. The Puritans were extremely isolated in their new community, and there was a great fear among members of being banished from the group. The Puritan community was a safe space, according to the leaders, and everything that was outside the community was outside of God's divine protection. This was helpful in keeping people from dissenting from within the community, because the fear of what was out there was far greater than whatever theological restraints were inside. This fear that held the community together was also a means of keeping others out of the community. Whether it is a small jungle community in South America, or a compound in the wilderness of Texas, isolation is key to bad theology. The Puritans left everything they knew and went to an underdeveloped, new land. Sure, the land was given to them by God, according to their leaders, but it was still frightening to think of the enemies (native peoples) who were waiting for them to leave the safe protection of the community. The fearmongering that took place via the Puritan leadership meant that the community embraced this isolationism. From their perspective, in their isolation they were living out their calling as God's chosen people in God's chosen land, and they were also protecting one another from the non-elect enemy that resided at every corner that wasn't part of their community. It made for a perfect echo chamber, and as we've discussed previously, any dissent was quickly taken care of.

What part did the everyday community members of the Puritan colony have in their own beliefs about theology? The answer appears to be very little. From the Old World of England to the New World of the colonies, Puritans were told very clearly and specifically what their theological beliefs were. These leaders, like Winthrop, were viewed as being the most important aspect of the new colony. For example, Winthrop preached his message of the elect and the promised land while simultaneously being made governor of the new colony. The religious leaders of the time were mayors, judges, ministers and so on; their word on the subject of theology was not to be challenged. The Puritans would not have had heated debates, discussions or Bible studies; instead, they had 3–4-hour sermons that would clearly lay out the groupthink of the community. This groupthink would have been focused on mirroring the story of the Israelites as they struggled to establish their city on a hill in the land that God had promised. How many sermons can one preach about the same subject? If you want that unquestioning belief in a singular cause, the answer is apparently quite a few.

Criterion 4 asks if there is any choice that you have in your theology, and it's quite clear that the general population was not consulted on the religious beliefs of the community at large. These religious beliefs influenced every aspect of life in the colony, and as a result there was a need for everyone to be on the same page. The leaders would have run a tight ship when it came to maintaining a common message in its theology, and that common message would have served their purpose of cohesion.

Criterion 5 relates to the idea that your theological belief is not focused on justice. When the Pequot were burning alive, the leadership made it clear that the Pequot deserved what was happening to them. Sometimes there must be violence, according to Mason; God demands it. The references to the Old Testament stories like Amalek justify the violent behavior of the Puritans against the native peoples. God demanded that everyone be destroyed in Amalek in order for God's covenant to continue to protect the children of Israel. Likewise, according to Winthrop, some non-chosen people may have to die in order to maintain the goodwill of God. The injustices of taking land, and even of murder, are not acknowledged by the Puritan leadership. Because the native peoples are not a part of the elect group, they are not seen as being worthy of the justice afforded within the community. According to the Puritans, injustice was only injustice if it occurred among those God has chosen.

Finally, criterion 6 is focused on the idea of equality. At the very core of the theology of election is inequality, whether it is divinely ordained or not. Election means that there are certain people who are in and there are others who are out. If you are outside the elect community, you are not just outside the community. Instead, if you are outside the community then you are not a part of God's chosen, and you are rather seen as an enemy of God's elect. This is especially so if you try and fight back against any injustice that you perceive to be true. Roger Williams wanted to pay the native peoples for their land and so he is banished as an unequal. The native peoples attempt to fight back against the colonists in order to fight the injustices that they see happening, and they are burned alive. There is no lamenting these banishings or these deaths. Those who are punished by the leadership of the Puritan community are seen as enemies of the divinely ordained. Because of the nature of the theology of election, inequality is an accepted feature of the divine hierarchy. There are some who are in and there are some who are out. However, the question remains: if you are out, is there hope for you? I would argue that it's hard to get to that conversation while you are taking all you can get from people and murdering those you see as less than you. Also, because of the high view of God's omniscience and grace in the theology of election, ultimately it is not the Puritans' job to bring people into the fold. That is a job for God and God alone. This understanding gets you off the hook of having any responsibility for the equality of those outside your divine community.

Notes

1 Alister McGrath, *Christian Theology: An Introduction*, 2nd edn (Oxford: Blackwell Publishing, 1997), pp. 449–57.
2 McGrath, *Christian Theology*, pp. 449–57.
3 McGrath, *Christian Theology*, pp. 449–57.
4 McGrath, *Christian Theology*, pp. 449–57.
5 See Perry Miller, *Errand into the Wilderness* (New York: Harper, 1956).

JOHN WINTHROP AND JOHN MASON

6 T. Walter Herbert, *Faith-Based War: From 9/11 to Catastrophic Success in Iraq* (London: Equinox, 2009).

7 Herbert, *Faith-Based War*, p. 31.

8 Jon Butler, Grant Wacker and Randall Balmer, *Religion in American Life: A Short History* (Oxford: Oxford University Press, 2007), p. 8.

9 The Puritans did lean towards Calvinist doctrines. For further discussion of the ways these doctrines were used in the USA, see Peter J. Thuesen, *Predestination: The American Career of a Contentious Doctrine* (Oxford: Oxford University Press, 2009).

10 John Winthrop, 'A Modell of Christian Charity (1630)', *Collections of the Massachusetts Historical Society* 3.7 (1838), pp. 31–48; Hanover Historical Texts Collection, https://history.hanover.edu/texts/winthmod.html (accessed 13.12.2019).

11 Winthrop, 'A Modell of Christian Charity'.

12 Winthrop, 'A Modell of Christian Charity'.

13 Winthrop, 'A Modell of Christian Charity'.

14 Winthrop, 'A Modell of Christian Charity'.

15 Winthrop, 'A Modell of Christian Charity'.

16 Winthrop, 'A Modell of Christian Charity'.

17 Herbert, *Faith-Based War*, p. 29.

18 Herbert, *Faith-Based War*, p. 32.

19 Anders Stephanson, *Manifest Destiny* (New York: Hill and Wang, 1995), p. 6.

20 Stephanson, *Manifest Destiny*, p. 7.

21 Herbert, *Faith-Based War*, p. 36.

22 John Mason, 'A Brief History of the Pequot War', *Humanities Web Website*, https://www.humanitiesweb.org/human.php?=n&p=1&ID=20 (accessed 30.8.2022).

23 Mason, 'A Brief History of the Pequot War'.

24 Mason, 'A Brief History of the Pequot War'.

25 Bradford in Herbert, *Faith-Based War*, p. 37.

26 Herbert, *Faith-Based War*, p. 37.

27 Underhill in Herbert, *Faith-Based War*, p. 37.

28 Underhill in Herbert, *Faith-Based War*, p. 37.

29 Williams in Herbert, *Faith-Based War*, p. 38.

30 Herbert, *Faith-Based War*, p. 40.

31 Herbert, *Faith-Based War*, p. 40.

32 Roger Finke and Rodney Stark, *The Churching of America (1776–2005)* (Piscataway, NJ: Rutgers University Press, 2008), p. 27.

33 Katherine Sonderegger, 'Election' in *The Oxford Handbook of Systematic Theology*, ed. John Webster, Kathryn Tanner and Iain Torrance (Oxford: Oxford University Press, 2007), p. 108.

6

The History of the Ku Klux Klan: A Bad Theology of Tradition

Theology and tradition

Tradition in the Christian church is controversial. Yes, you heard that right. Controversial. Aren't we expecting that at this stage? But instead of being in the 'bad' theology category, what we see is that tradition in its 'good' sense is still within the boundaries of controversial. Tradition is important to those who are a part of the Christian community. It is important because it helps to define people, boundaries, rituals, activities, and even understandings of the Christian sacred text. Some people who are Christian are born into these traditions. Some are born into them but leave for other ones. Some Christians find their own way into certain traditions. Because traditions define us, they can also at times divide us. We will get to the division later, but in the meantime it is important to see tradition as a systematic theological idea that works with the interpretation of scripture and the passing of history in order to move the Christian religion along as a community. In its most 'good' form it is a community-builder, and it is that community-building that will be focus of this section.

According to A. N. Williams:

> tradition represents communal interpretation of the Bible which is above all, though not exclusively, doctrinal in content. The vast majority of commentators moreover specify that tradition's relation to the Bible is derivative, and in that

sense, tradition is secondary in authoritative status, though it can still be regarded as normative: tradition is the *norma normans* (the rule that stipulates) while scripture is the *norma normans non normata* (the rule that stipulates but is not stipulated by any other rule than itself).[1]

This definition is confusing even to those who study theology (the Latin doesn't help), but what we are seeing here is wrestling between the influence of human interpretation and the authority of scripture that occurs with some systematic theologians. Tradition is a human endeavour, and the author of this definition isn't willing to admit otherwise, but if there is a human element then where does the text stand as an unmovable standard (if you believe in the inherency of the Bible)? And even if you don't believe the Bible is the word of God exactly, and humans dictate tradition, then wherein does the authority lie for claiming a tradition as true or accurate?

For the sake of this book, we do not have to wrestle with these systematic ideas. We can instead look at tradition as an 'is.' The brilliance of Practical Theology is that while we are called to look at injustices in theology as 'what could be', in the case of simply defining systematic ideas we can at times say that things 'are' in Christian theology. In the case of tradition, we can look around our world and see that there are groups of communities of Christians who do things differently. While I will say that the Ku Klux Klan has a bad theology of tradition (and specifically Protestantism), it is not my place to say that Protestantism in other forms is more 'true' than other traditions. Instead, it is a distinct tradition in Christian history, and if it follows the criteria of good theology then it can fall within that category, of course.

But why is there such contention about this particular systematic idea as being true or right? You do see this with other systematic ideas, where different theologians will present alternative views on things like eschatology, election or providence. And while they might claim desperately that their ideas are right and true, those theological debates do not seem to hold the same weight as the debates around tradition. This relates directly to the way that the place of scripture (and interpretation of scripture) is seen in tradition. Therefore, from the beginning there was a need for a normative interpretation of scripture. Something that could guide the church in the right way to understand and 'do' the Christian tradition once Jesus and the original disciples were all gone.

For the first years of the Christian church, tradition served as a primary means of avoiding falling apart as a community. What was holy and what was heretical was determined by church leaders, and they guided followers in what to do and how and when. Within tradition there must be a form of power – a place from which the answers come on how to be Christian. In the early years of the Christian church that power came from leaders, and there was little questioning. It seems from the beginning of the Christian tradition that it was the leaders and their theological interpretations that determined what we know as tradition today. As a result, tradition is sometimes seen as being one's theological position (as interpreted from the text) or even the Christian denomination that one chooses. These things can be, and are usually, related.

The Roman Catholic Church is seen as the continuation of the traditions of the early church. It became an established religion in the Roman Empire in AD 313, under Constantine. Following a series of councils (where theology for the church was confirmed and established as true), the church began to split. The tradition had become traditions, and it would remain that way until this day. As the Reformation came around, this understanding of where the power of tradition lies was challenged even further. In the sixteenth century across Europe, the Reformers declared that it was not the people of the church who should decide what tradition might look like, but scripture alone. This was a challenge to the Catholic/Orthodox church and the way it viewed leadership and power (among other issues). In many ways, the Christian tradition up to this point had been the leadership and the church itself, and so the

Reformers could have been seen as destroying the idea of tradition with their desires to return to the text to start anew.

Some believed there could be no reliance on scripture to guide the Christian church because there was no one interpretation of the text that was not sanctioned by some ecclesial body. According to Williams, the early church fathers Tertullian and Irenaeus did not see a means by which scripture alone could guide anyone. In the view of those early church fathers, 'scripture is simply apostolic tradition in written form'.[2] It was an admirable goal to try and see the sacred text of the Christian religion as being the sole guide, but ultimately the diversity in interpretation represented as a stumbling block. At the Council of Trent, the Roman Catholic Church clarified its position on the relationship between scripture and tradition. According to Williams, the Council upheld that there are two different places where revelation in the Christian community might come: tradition and scripture. Further councils in the Catholic tradition debated this idea, and also came through with their own ideas. In Vatican II it was declared that scripture and tradition come from the same divine source, and as such they both are mutually beneficial and should be respected. And while scripture and revelation are important sources of divine inspiration, Vatican II declared that one needed the 'living teaching office of the church' to give an 'authentic interpretation'.[3] This sealed the importance of the leadership in the Catholic Church to the overall understanding of the Christian tradition.

Even the reformers had some doctrines that they chose to keep despite any discrepancies with the scriptural tradition. The idea of the Trinity, for instance, remained in place despite its lack of explicit content in the sacred text. This in itself could showcase how some theological understandings can become tradition or normalized as history moves forward. But these theological ideas are few and far between, and while they may represent some big ideas in the Christian tradition that remain steadfast, they certainly don't cover the whole theological spectrum. As a result, we see theological conflicts in the reformed tradition from the very beginning. These conflicts, though, were in no way comparable with the councils that split some aspects of the Catholic Church. These conflicts in the reformed churches caused split after split after split. It came to the point where one didn't have to be born into a tradition, but instead could pick and choose what version of Christianity one might want to be a part of in the vast number of Protestant churches. As long as it was scripture alone, there were going to be different people interpreting it, and as a result there was an endless supply of different denominations or traditions to choose from.

It also appears that tradition is evolving and expanding in its scope as history moves forward. One might only look to the post-Vatican II theological contributions. These theological developments were called 'contextual' by many in the Christian community. I take particular offence to this title, as it implies that there is non-contextual theology. If we see anything from our discussion so far about tradition, it is that tradition is inherently contextual. The Peruvian anthropologist and missiologist Tito Paredes discusses this idea further. He uses the helpful analogy of the Christian sacred text and teachings as being like a seed. Paredes argues that when foreign missionaries went to Latin America, they brought the 'seed' as a flower, and not just a 'full-grown flower' but a 'flower in a particular flower pot'. He suggested that the only way for the gospel to grow in this new land was to plant it in the local soil, and let it become a part of the actual floral landscape of the countries that it was being brought to. According to Paredes: 'It was presumed that the ecclesiastical tradition that was brought was normative and biblical and that there was no need to question or alter it.'[4]

While Christians may not like to admit it, tradition has been challenged from the very beginning of Christian history. The Jerusalem Council that took place in AD 50 was established to clarify rules for Gentiles converting to Christianity. This was a clarification that needed to happen because the message of Jesus and the early church was adapting to different contexts, and as a result of this adaptation there was a need to clarify certain theological aspects of the community. The reason there is such a controversial tone around discussions of tradition is that there is a push and pull between the tendency of theology to adapt to time and place, and the tendency for people to want to have a one true authority on what is accurate in the Christian community. 'Contextual' theology must be labelled as such because there has to be an authority that is universal in Christianity; someone who has the one real answer to the question of the scriptural message that has been left to humans.

The result of this need, especially in the USA, is that you get versions of scriptural interpretation that are spoken about as though they are the ultimate authority. In this book I have showcased a great number of examples of this exact phenomenon. But the human need for that authoritative voice and certain religious groups' ability to translate scripture to fit their own belief system means that bad theology occurs. Tradition is not immune to bad theology, as we will analyse in the following sections. The Protestant tradition that was trying so hard to fight against a powerful tradition in the Catholic Church continued to change and evolve as it moved through history. In most of these situations globally, that was not an issue, but in the case of the Ku Klux Klan it was used as a means of justifying hate towards other people. Protesting they were, but to what ends?

History of the Ku Klux Klan in the USA

> Because men and women are God's creatures, some of their culture is rich in beauty and goodness. Because they are fallen, all of it is tainted with sin ... Missions have all too frequently exported with the gospel an alien culture and churches have sometimes been in bondage to culture rather than to Scripture.[5]

One thing that is important to note about the Ku Klux Klan (KKK) is that there is no one clear history of the organization. There are three very distinct time periods where they were most active, and these are the periods that have been most studied by scholars. The mythology of the modern-day Ku Klux Klan developed in the story of Leo Frank and a young girl named Mary Phagan. In 1913, Phagan was a 13-year-old white girl from Marietta in Georgia. In the summer of that year, she travelled to the local pencil factory where she worked, and never returned. The nightwatchmen found the young girl dead at the factory. Phagan became a star in the local paper because of her whiteness, her innocence and the fact that she was local. Understandably, the media demanded justice for the girl. Several suspects were brought in for questioning, but ultimately the Atlanta police focused in on one: Leo Frank. Frank was a Jew from up north, and was also the manager of the pencil factory at the time of Phagan's death. A fellow worker in the factory, Jim Conley, testified against Frank, saying that he had made sexual advances to other young women at the factory. Conley was an African American, and he admitted moving Phagan's body under Frank's order.

Frank was convicted in August 1913 of Phagan's murder, and given a life sentence in prison. The governor during the trial, William Slaton, had his doubts about the witness testimony against Frank, and this is ultimately how Leo Frank got life in prison and not a death sentence. The citizens of Georgia, however, were not as convinced of Frank's innocence, and created a mythology around Phagan that depicted her with almost angelic qualities. Songs were created in her honour, and they highlighted that Frank might not suffer in this life, but he would certainly pay his dues in the next. The 'Knights of Mary Phagan' emerged during this time, and they were composed of local men who believed that justice had not been served in the case of Phagan's trial. They decided to take matters into their own hands, and in August 1915, 25 men attacked the jail where Leo Frank was being held. They kidnapped Frank and brought him to Marietta, where they lynched him in front of a crowd. Many local people saw this as a victory for justice for Mary Phagan, but others across the country were horrified. Many historians who study the KKK view the Knights of

Mary Phagan as the first incarnation of later, more organized, versions of the Ku Klux Klan.

The original KKK, as people have come to know it, was formed in the reconstruction period of the civil war. This period is represented by the time where both the north and the south were adjusting to their new reality post-slavery. Needless to say, many confederate soldiers were less than pleased at the outcome of the civil war and felt as though the north was imposing its own views and ways of life on a defeated south. In their view, these ways of life were being implemented in the southern states too quickly.

It was out of this atmosphere that the first KKK came to be. Comprised mostly of veterans of the civil war, the first Klan began in Tennessee in 1865. According to KKK documents, the Ku Klux part of the name came from the Greek, *kyklos*, which means circle. The Klan aspect was supposedly a reference to the connection between the community and their Scottish roots. According to William Simmons (the first KKK leader), the South was humiliated in the reconstruction era. Simmons states that the KKK began in this time period due to the

> urgent necessities of the reconstruction period. [At the end] of the War between the States, the South was prostrated and devastation spread from the Potomac to the Rio Grande ... Negros everywhere were organized and taught to hate white people of the Southern states. [This] alien race, untaught, unskilled and incapable of government [preyed upon the properties and the homes of these] white men of the South who had borne arms in the defense of the confederacy.[6]

This gross fear-mongering was perpetuated throughout the south, and it was widely believed to be true. Part of the reason why the community in the south believed rumours like this was that those who were perpetuating the fear were Christian ministers. Local ministers who the community trusted were recruited as the front line of the KKK, and they would remain in that position as important allies of relaying 'reliable' Klan information to the general public.

By 1867, there were regional groups of the KKK that were meeting on a regular basis. They called themselves the 'Invisible Empire of the South', and became more formalized in the way that they operated. No longer were they just a group of disgruntled, ex-military who aired grievances. They now had leadership who they called 'grand wizards', who oversaw more local leadership known as 'grand dragons', 'grand cyclops' and 'grand titans'. The first of these grand wizards was an ex-confederate soldier, Nathan Bedford Forrest. (On a personal note, when I was being awarded my undergraduate degree in Rome, Georgia (USA), I saw a very large statue dedicated to Forrest in the town centre. It has since been removed and taken to the history museum in the area.)

The Klan spread rapidly throughout the south, and throughout the whole of the USA. By 1870, there were branches of the KKK in almost every southern state. The first incarnation of the Klan was hyper-focused on reinstating the status quo in the south – that is, white supremacy. So while the KKK's actions were not always coordinated, their goal was very clear. They would attack any institution or situation that was encouraging the equality of black people to that of white people, especially in the south. They adopted their white robes and their hoods in order to further their campaign of intimidation, as well as to offer a form of protection from identification. The first version of the KKK was violent from the beginning. It had a singular focus, and it was willing to kill in order to restore the supremacy of whites in the region. In a typically cowardly fashion they were particularly strong in areas where the black population was low; and it was in those areas where the KKK was particularly active that people of colour suffered the most violence. A hotbed of KKK activity was in South Carolina, where in one night in 1871 eight black people were lynched in Union County.

One of the key misrepresentations of the Klan is that their community was comprised of mostly poor, uneducated, fringe southerners. While this is an easier narrative to spin in terms of explaining the violent and hateful behaviour of the Klan, it does not represent the actual composition of the group. One would hope that the KKK would be a fringe group, and not something that represented the whole of the USA. However, what we see is that this was not the case. From the very beginning, the KKK had representatives from all walks of life, and we especially see this in the 1920s incarnation of the group. This proliferation of the Klan across socioeconomic boundaries was so real during the reconstruction era that police officers were either members of the KKK or reluctant to prosecute members of the group. Even if the police did manage to get members of the Klan to the stage of prosecution for their crimes, they could rarely find witnesses to testify against them. So while members of society might not be active in the KKK community, they were willing (or scared enough) to keep their mouths shut when it was attempted to bring members of the KKK to justice.

In the end, the violence became too much. The reconstructed KKK were out of control in terms of their scope of violence. A recent report from the Equal Justice Initiative estimates that from 1865 to 1876 there were 2,000 racially motivated lynchings of black people (including men, women and children).[7] Republicans, at the time the pro-freedom party for the slaves, went to Congress to try and get something done about the killings. In 1871, the Ku Klux Klan Act was passed. This Act offered extended federal protection to freed slaves and those who aided them in their endeavours of equality. It declared that certain offences being committed by the KKK were federal offences, and that they could be prosecuted as such. These offences included intimidation of people who have the right to hold office, participate in their civil duties and who are trying to participate in activities that are rights for any person who is an equal citizen in the USA. Violations of this Act could result in federal forces being sent to enforce the laws. There was some outrage surrounding these developments, but essentially it quelled the active white supremacy perpetuated by the

KKK at the time. The Klan had been quieted for a while, but that quiet would not last for long.

The KKK of the 1920s

As lore goes, the second incarnation of the KKK began with William J. Simmons and a dream. Simmons was a former Methodist minister who was stripped of his ordination in 1912. The dream in question consisted of a 'row of horses seemed to be galloping across the horizon ... [their riders were] white robed figures ... a rough outline of the United States appeared as the background'.[8] Simmons immediately fell to the ground and began to pray. As he lay there, he promised that he would figure out how to fix the issues that troubled the USA, as well as highlight the heroism of the previous KKK. He believed that the current climate of the period from 1915 to the 1930s, his divine vision, and his fond memories of the original Klan meant that he was supposed to re-create the KKK in a new context.

But what could change the notion that people by now had of the Ku Klux Klan? Simmons' answer was simple: religion. It is for this reason that the second KKK is the snapshot for this chapter. While religion was implied in the first incarnation, and assumed in the civil rights KKK, the true theological developments of the KKK took place in this second version of the group. Simmons founded the new incarnation of the KKK on Stone Mountain, Georgia, on Thanksgiving Day 1915 with 19 of his fellow 'Knights'. The Knights set fire to a cross on top of Stone Mountain and declared the Ku Klux Klan alive once again. According to Kelly J. Baker, the new Klan was in some ways the same as ever, but with a new emphasis:

> But what is missing is not the 1920s Klan's dedication to nation, the rights of white men, and the vulnerability of white women but the prominent place of religion, specifically Protestant Christianity ... Simmons was formerly a minister

who created a new Klan firmly enshrouded in the language of Protestantism.[9]

This version of the Klan was not just a group that was called by God to protect the status quo – it was also a religious order that was on a campaign to defend Protestantism in the USA.

In some ways, the 1920s focus on Protestantism fits with previous ideas that the Klan put forth in their print culture. This version of the KKK was simply clothed in religious imagery. Simmons, the founder and former minister, was quickly usurped by a new leader, Hiram Wesley Evans. Evans continued with the message of the previous KKK: anti-Jewish, anti-black, anti-Catholic, pro-American, pro-Protestant, pro-education. At a meeting of the Grand Dragons, Evans claimed the following about the KKK mission:

> [it is] a Holy Cause so far blessed with the support of the Almighty God ... [that was brought about by] men of dependable character and sterling worth who were able to lend some kind of concrete form to the God-given idea destined to again save a white man's civilization ... [the new creation of the Klan was] formed, aided, supported, guided, and directed by Almighty God in the working out of his invisible purposes and mighty decrees.[10]

Unlike in its other incarnations, the 1920s Klan really worked to show people that their cause was deeply connected to the overall purposes of God.

What were the causes that the 1920s Klan justified by their theological beliefs? Unlike previous and consequent incarnations of the KKK, this version of the Klan represented the beliefs of a great number of American citizens. Yes, the Klan used religion, but it also used social issues that were troubling some people in the USA at the time. Far from being just a fringe movement, the 1920s Klan had a large membership that transcended geography and socioeconomic factors. The media portrait of the Klan portrayed them as being a far-right group that had very few adherents. In reality:

that portrait sidelined the Klan to the margins of American history despite its large membership and cultural influence. By labeling the order as a fringe movement of terrorists, the nefarious elements of the movement appear in historical narratives without exploration of its broader appeal to white Protestants.[11]

It was easier to think that this version of the Klan did not represent the ideals of the USA at the time, but this doesn't appear to be the case. The 1920s had a series of perceived threats that this version of the Klan locked into. First, there was the perceived, ever-present threat from Jewish and Catholic groups in the USA. The KKK saw the Jews as being a direct enemy of God, because of their perceived continuous defiance of God's wishes in the Old Testament. The Catholics were perceived as serving the Pope and the Catholic Church above all else, thus they would not be able to fully serve the American cause. Women's rights were also starting to emerge during this period, which contradicted the KKK's traditional understanding of a woman's place being in the home.

There were other perceived enemies, specifically African American males in the USA, who they saw as being a particular threat against white women. Immigrants were also viewed with the utmost suspicion, because of the un-Americanism that they could bring to the USA. Historians see these 'enemies' as being indicative of a lot of fears in the USA at the time, not just a fringe viewpoint. They have analysed the understandings of the 1920s Klan alongside other popular print culture that was available at the time, and there are similarities. Some scholars see the Klan as being a conservative movement in the midst of a number of other conservative movements at the time, including the American Legion and the Daughters of the American Revolution.

A final threat, but a very real one, was the threat that the Klan saw in relation to the next generation. With the inclusion of immigrants and non-Protestant, non-white, males into the classroom, there was a perceived fear that the next generation would not be as sympathetic to the Klan's cause. There was also a fear that the young people would not be American in the way that they should be – that is, Protestant and white, with traditional family values. As a result, one of the campaigns the Klan were quick to advocate for was the inclusion of prayer and Bibles in state schools. The Klan would hold rallies to convince parents that their children were being corrupted by the education system. The founding fathers maybe wanted separation of church and state, but according to the Klan they never intended that religion should be completely banished from the state school system.

Despite all of these social issues that seemed to be guiding the group, the underpinning compass of the Klan's beliefs remained religious. Baker adds:

> Understanding the central role of religion helps scholars understand better the motivations and appeal of those movements beyond simplistic presentations of frustration and anger, which remain popular excuses for memberships in such movements. *Moreover, examining movements like the Klan also suggests the ways that religion can inform ideologies of intolerance, violence, and terror, as well as bolster the commitment of members by relying on a more ultimate cause for such insidious agendas.*[12]

The Klan of the 1920s had branches across the USA, not just the rural south. There were upwards of four million members of the Klan by 1925. Clearly, this was not a group small in number, but instead the Klan was latching itself on to the unspoken fear that found itself perpetuated across the USA in the middle classes and beyond.

It should be noted here that Kelly Baker, who has written extensively about the Klan, has similar feelings about good and bad religion. She laments the fact that historians refuse to acknowledge the religiosity of the KKK during the 1920s incarnation. She says, and I agree, that by putting religion into categories of true and false religion, we aren't helping to analyse the religious beliefs that the Klan had during this time. She offers the following:

> Other scholarship argues that the religion of the Klan and other hate movements was patently 'false' religion. This tiresome declaration of false religion obscured the commitment of members to the religious vision of the order and marginalized the centrality of that vision to the Klan's appeal. The order relied on religious systems ranging from a white supremacist version of Protestantism in the 1920s to today's Christian Identity movement.[13]

Much like my own project, Baker agrees that setting up a dichotomy of true and false religion does nothing to further the field of religious studies in these scenarios. She goes on to say:

> If they [the Klan] are not authentically religious, then their motivations are not impacted by religion at all. Second and more important, presenting the religion of the Klan as false religion allows an assumption that religion is somehow not associated with movements and people who might be unsavory, disreputable, or dangerous. Religion is at its best ambiguous, which means that it can be associated with movements we label 'good' or 'bad,' but limiting the place of religion does not mean that religion, specifically Christianity, cannot be associated with the Klan ...[14]

This has been a conclusion that we have examined throughout this book, and I believe Baker puts it in a way that showcases the importance of viewing these movements as religious and not just dismissing this aspect of their justification. 'True or false, legitimate or illegitimate, the Klan still upheld its Protestantism',[15] according to Baker. Amen, says Leah Robinson.

From the perspective of recruitment, the Klan used religious justification and Americanism to underpin the present fears of the American people about Jews, Catholics, African Americans, women and immigrants. A further recruiting tool was incorporated into the 1920s Klan's plan for a nationwide community. The KKK began to publish media that pushed the idea that if a man was not a part of the organization, he was not a masculine man. Women were portrayed as defenceless and vulnerable, and men were seen as the ultimate protectors in this world. As a result, to be a successful member of the KKK one had to be a Protestant, a protector, and also masculine. The flip side of this recruiting tool was that any male who was white and Protestant but not a part of the KKK was, accordingly, not masculine. If American men were committed to patriotism and defending the way of the USA, they had to be a part of the group. The Klan even began to use the phrase of 'destiny' for those who joined the organization: 'That destiny included more than patriotic duty. It also included uniformity in (Protestant) Christianity and white supremacy. The Anglo-Saxon heritage of the Klan, and of America, directly resulted in the greatness of the nation ...'[16] This pressure for recruiting was very clear in the printed media, which was passed around (even in churches).

There is a lot of public KKK media with regard to the hatred that the Klan had for anyone they viewed as the 'other'. I have tried to stick closely to the religious aspects of many of these descriptions, but it is worth noting that while the KKK justified their antisemitism by the perceived defiance of the Jews against God in the Old Testament, their hatred of the African American population was very focused on non-religious racism. In the KKK magazine called the *Menace*, there is a description of the way the Klan viewed the 'Negro'. The magazine stated, as though fact, that the 'low mentality of the savage ancestors [coursed through the veins] of the colored race in America'.[17] Further, Simmons stated that 'Negroes' spoke to one another in the 'jargon of the jungle [and they were] one generation removed from savagery'.[18] The Klan simply did not believe that African-Americans were capable of citizenship in the USA at the same level as the white community. They feared the progress that was taking place with regard to the rights of African Americans in the USA, and they were deeply against the idea that white people would share basic rights with people of colour. The KKK called African Americans a problem, and they only saw three options to solve it: slavery, extermination and amalgamation.[19] Leaders in the Klan decided that going back to slavery was probably not going to happen, so that particular option was out. Extermination was not a possibility, not because it was genocide but because they saw the African Americans as breeding too fast to keep up. The last option was simply not possible to the KKK because it went against everything they believed in terms of mixing the highest race of purity with that of a lower race.

One might ask what the overall concern was with the 'other' that the Klan seemed to be obsessed with. They had their theological/social reasons for hating those who were not like themselves, but what was the root of some of these beliefs? It seems as though the KKK was concerned about their place in society in the USA. The KKK would hold rallies that encouraged communities to get back to their 'roots', and the roots of their founders. According to the Klan, the founders were white, male, Protestant and pro-American. There was a need, then, to return to this world where these men were in charge of everything, and where they were at the top of the food chain in the USA. Equal rights, immigration and religious plurality; all these made the Klan feel as though they were losing power in their own land. And not only that, but what they saw as the true America was getting watered down by the influx of 'others' and the lifting up of 'others' into positions of equality.

However, this mentality would not last for ever, and by 1930 the membership of the KKK had dropped significantly. Controversies in leadership and general public resistance changed the status of the 1920s KKK, and they were no longer seen as some type of pro-American, fraternal organization. They instead were seen as a racist, hate group, which diminished their popularity significantly. In 1925 there were some two to five million members, but by 1930 there were around 30,000. One would have hoped that the nation might have seen the error of its ways, and that this is what led to the decline of the Klan. This was not the case, though, and the decline is seemingly related to the solidification of the bias that the Klan perpetuated in American society by the 1930s. The idea that there needed to be an organization that would enforce ideas of inequality felt redundant in this time period. That white, Protestant males needed an organization to further their power also seemed a redundant notion, and as a result the Klan became unnecessary. The numbers dwindled as its message of hatred was codified in the culture. The second incarnation eventually dwindled and faded out even as their ideas became the fabric of American society.

The KKK of the Civil Rights Movement (and beyond)

In the postwar years, the Klan again emerged, this time fighting against the Civil Rights Movement that was sweeping across the USA. Again, we see the importance of the 1920s Klan to the later incarnations of the KKK. While the post-civil war Klan had the specific cause of restoring the old South, the 1920s Klan fleshed out the actual institution and gave it a more theologically based purpose and mission. The 1960s Klan used these ideas to further their battle against the progress being made by African Americans throughout the nation. What we do notice about the Klan during this time is that they do not have the unified backing of many millions within the USA like they did in the 1920s. The KKK in the 1960s and beyond moved to individual splinter groups in various areas of the USA. They used the previous incarnation's doctrines, mission and outfits, but their status as a united organization was all but non-existent.

This does not mean that they were not effective in their quest for violence against those who were looking for progress in the USA. This version of the Klan was going public with their violence. They knew they no longer could simply publish their ideas, but they had to actually defend those ideas in the public realm. The Civil Rights Movement was changing the face of the south at a rapid rate, and it gave fuel to the fragments of the Klan that dotted the country. There were numerous murders that took place during the third incarnation of the Klan. Some of the best-known include the 1951 bombing of the home of the NAACP activists Harry and Harriette Moore, the 1963 assassination of the Civil Rights activist Medgar Evars, and the 16th Street Baptist Church bombing that killed four African American girls – Addie Mae Collins, Cynthia Wesley, Carole Robertson and Carol Denise McNair.

Theologically, this Klan was less inclined to project their Christian beliefs on to their activities. They held to the Klan's beliefs of the 1920s but were far more focused on correcting the perceived social ills of the 1960s and 1970s. The 'Christian Identity' understanding of the Klan was solidified during this incarnation. As we have seen, this theological justification of white supremacy had become very popular in the 1920s, and continued on through further Klan incarnations. Christian Identity theology believes that the white race are the actual descendants of the Israelites. Non-whites are from the line of Cain and are cursed as a result (this was a common notion in the period of slavery as well). Non-white people will for ever be a lesser race in the eyes of those who practise this particular religious interpretation. In fact, those who adhere to this theology believe that non-whites will eventually be enslaved to the white people in the kingdom of God on earth.

There were attempts to unite the various fractions of the KKK during the 1960s, but these were unsuccessful. By 1964, the Klan was under investigation by Congress. The numbers in the Klan declined, at least on paper, as members were forced to testify in front of Congress. As the USA made ideas about equal rights into law, the Klan continued to lose members, reaching a low point in membership in 1974 (1,500). They were designated a hate group by the Southern Poverty Law Center, and it seemed as though the Klan's days of being a force in the USA were over. This applied until 2015 when membership began steadily to increase again. They remained splintered, but these splintered groups were gaining followers. According to reports, the number of Klan chapters across the USA grew from 72 to 190 in 2015.

In 2022, John Blake released an article on CNN.com titled: 'An "imposter Christianity" is threatening American Democracy'.[20] The article discussed the insurrection in Washington DC on 6 January. It talked about how people who participated in this rally held banners, or chanted words that came from the Christian Identity theology that was held so dear by the KKK. At the rally we heard that the USA was a Christian nation that was founded on Protestant, Christian beliefs. Quoted in the article is Yale University's Philip Gorski, who states that this idea is 'half truth, a mythological version of American history'.[21] The author of the article goes so far as to say that this understanding of American history is 'bad history and bad theology'.[22]

Blake also points out that many people who participated on 6 January were producing information that suggested that Jesus was a warrior and a fighter. This is a common idea in the world of the Klan, who see that their religious beliefs and their theology mean that they have to go into the world and act for their cause. These actions look different in the different incarnations, but it was none the less present. Blake also goes on to consider the common Klan idea that was discussed on 6 January. This was the idea of 'real' Americans, or those who deserve to be able to dictate what happens in the country at the expense of others who are not authentically American. Further conversations that are beginning to circulate in the far right relate to the importance of education. Education should produce model, American citizens (in a very traditional sense of course).

The Klan did not just discuss their bad theology in public forums. They also codified their bad theology into theological doctrine. They have thus developed a Doctrinal Statement of Beliefs that can be found on many official Klan websites. The first part of these documents reads fairly standard as 'We believes' go. There is a great deal of repeating of this doctrine in relation to the importance of the Old Testament, Jesus' divinity and the role of Jesus' death in the overall message of the Christian faith. With that out of the way, however, things start to take a turn. About halfway through their declaration there is the following: 'We believe God chose unto Himself a special race of people that are above all people upon the face of the earth (Deut. 7.6; Amos 3.2).'[23] This statement goes on to explain that instead of the Jews being the Children of Israel, it is actually:

> White, Anglo-Saxon, Germanic and kindred people [who are] God's true, literal Children of Israel. Only this race fulfills every detail of Biblical Prophecy and World History concerning Israel and continues in these latter days to be heirs and possessors of the Covenants, Prophecies, Promises and Blessings YHVH God made to Israel.[24]

The Doctrinal Statement of Beliefs creates a scenario where the white race is the actual chosen people of God. Enemy number one in the Statement is the Jewish race. Historically, Jews were known as the chosen people of God. According to the Klan's doctrines, however, this status has dramatically changed for the Jews: 'We believe in an existing being known as the Devil or Satan and the Serpent (Gen. 3.1; Rev. 12.9) who has a literal "seed" or posterity in the earth (Gen. 3.15) commonly called Jews today (Rev. 2.9; 3.9; Isa. 65.15).'[25]

A bad theology of tradition

> The Klan, in its founding, bound Christianity with American-ism and members' professed allegiance to both despite their relentless critics. In the order's white Protestant America, the order envisioned not only that members were the defenders of Protestant Christianity, but also that God had a direct hand in the creation of the order.[26]

While there is a multitude of theological analysis that could be done with regard to bad theology in the KKK, I am choosing to analyse their understanding of tradition. As was discussed in the first section, tradition as a systematic term can be problematic even without a hate group being involved. The questions about what is true or accurate, or even real-life talk about God, are always going to cause division. This division at its best cultivates like-minded communities of theological creativity and common worship and rites/rituals. At its worst, these communities can create an us versus them mentality, and this is where the bad theology of tradition in the KKK falls.

The Klan claims an ultimate knowledge of the ways and intentions of God on earth, and as a result they claim to know what tradition is accurately representing the mind of God – Protestantism. Protestantism in itself, as the history goes, is not inherently a hateful tradition. It was a tradition that began as a means of challenging the status quo of the church at the time. As time moved forward, this tradition continued to develop (and split), and different Christian communities were formed that had their own unique understanding of the Protestant tradition. The Klan latched on to this tradition, not any denomination in particular (though there were ones they distrusted more), and they created an us versus them mentality in relation to anyone who was not a part of that tradition (among other things).

In relation to criterion 1, your theology is being used to limit the flourishing of humans – where to begin? The first Klan emerged at the end of the civil war as a means of protesting the progress that was taking place in the black community at the time. By the second incarnation of the Klan, there were further theological articulations of how the Jews were not from the line of the original Israelites. The Klan believed that Jews were from an alternative line, and as a result were a lesser race than the white people. While some might look at this and see the Klan as using a false religion, I am on Kelly Baker's side on this argument. I do not see this as being helpful in the overall discussion of religious studies. Whether they were religious or not is of no consequence to me. As a Practical Theologian I am interested in what they did with their theological understandings in practice, and in this case they tried desperately to limit the flourishing of anyone who was not white and Protestant. Not only did they try and create an us versus them mentality with the black community, but they also intimidated people of colour from embracing a new-found freedom after the civil war and beyond. They did this through words, threats and violence with the sole goal of limiting their flourishing. This extends to other people of colour, immigrants, Jews, Catholics and women. Their theology was built on the idea that white, male, Protestants were at the top of the food chain and, as a result, the 'flourishing' of any other group was theologically the opposite of what they believed.

In terms of criterion 2, self-reflection, we can see that there is very little with regard to reflection in the Klan. Perhaps the only version of reflection we see is when the second incarnation of the Klan tried to move away from what they saw as the negative press around the violence of the first incarnation. The second Klan tried to develop a more complex theological justification for their actions, so they would be able to recruit in a more open way. In other words, they wanted the everyday person in the USA not to feel as though they were joining a hate organization but that they were truly joining a fraternity of like-minded individuals. That reflection, however, is not at all about their beliefs or actions; instead, it was about how to get the middle class in the USA into their organization. There is no reflection on their theological conclusions at all. They stay firmly in the belief that they are a master race that is truly American.

Criterion 3 is the favourite of all of those who are operating under the banner of bad theology. Creating an us versus them mentality is the basis of the theology of the Klan. From their 'We believes' we see the following:

We believe the White, Anglo-Saxon, Germanic and kindred people to be God's true, literal Children of Israel. Only this race fulfills every detail of Biblical Prophecy and World History concerning Israel and continues in these latter days to be heirs and possessors of the Covenants, Prophecies, Promises and Blessings YHVH God made to Israel.[27]

From the language of 'only this race', there is already an establishment of us versus them. And not only is there an us versus them, but there is also an 'us is better than them' mentality that inherently creates discrimination. In the case of the Klan there is an us versus them that is based on something that can't be changed: race. So from the beginning we see their theological beliefs as being discriminatory in a way that can't be changed, and as a result there will for ever be the 'them' status. Not only are they 'them', but they are a theologically evil 'them' in a way that cannot be changed. According again to their 'We believes': 'We believe in an existing being known as the Devil or Satan and the Serpent (Gen. 3.1; Rev. 12.9) who has a literal "seed" or posterity in the earth (Gen. 3.15) commonly called Jews today (Rev. 2.9; 3.9; Isa. 65.15).'[28] As a result, the 'them' is an evil 'them' who must be defeated in order to save the USA – an evil you cannot escape or convert from, but which is the very essence of someone (whether that is a person of colour, a Jewish person, a Catholic person, or a woman, for instance).

Much like criterion 3, criterion 4 states that your theological understandings isolate you from other people or from groups of people. Clearly, the Klan used theology to create an us versus them mentality, but as was mentioned under criterion 3 above, this isolation cannot be escaped easily. This is not just a 'convert to a religion' and 'join a group' type of theology. The Klan's theology says there are God-ordained differences in communities of people, and there is little means by which you can change. As a result, there is an isolation from anyone who doesn't fit into your very thin definition of those who have been blessed by God. Not only are you isolated from 'others' who don't fit into your theological conclusions, but you are also violently opposed to those who do not fit into your world view. The Klan does this actively. They are a hate group, and as a result they hate those who do not fit into the white, Protestant community. This is directly related to maintaining power dynamics, but it is also clothed in theological language to justify it.

Some Klan members who have defected have done so because of the unchanging mentality of the group. Protestantism has always been the cornerstone of the Klan. If you do not believe Protestant rites/rituals/ways of church, then you are already unable to be a part of the group. In this there is no negotiation. The Catholic Church is inherently evil and is not a part of God's will for humanity. In the second incarnation of the Klan there was an adoption of certain Christian rituals, like baptism into KKK initiations. This caused some members to call out the Klan as being blasphemous. To these defectors, it is one thing to say you are a Christian fraternity with a singular cause, but it is quite another to imitate the *actual* Christian church. This did not deter the Klan in what they were doing or how they did it. In fact, if anything it caused the Klan to write down and solidify their theological 'We believes'. Once these were adopted, they were not changed. Much like certain denominations within the Christian church, any change in theological beliefs is seen as uncertainty or weakness. As a result, there is little to no choice in changing or adapting any of the theological beliefs of the Klan, even if you are a part of the community. The ideas have been established by leadership, and they remain steadfast; you either accept it or you are out (immediately a 'them').

Criterion 5 is interesting in the sense of the focus on justice. You have the interpretations from within the Klan that suggest that they see their theological beliefs as being heavily focused on the justice of the group. This, according to the Klan, is justice that is based on God's divine order, and as a result any actions in relation to pushing back against 'others' is justified. Social justice in relation to what is seen as liberal ideas is brushed aside as being something that is not coming from God, but coming from the devil. According to the Klan, there is a clear social structure, and any social justice initiatives that attempt to progress causes that are not related to the divine structure are human endeavours and not from God. So while those outside the Klan may see the group as hateful and working towards injustice, the Klan would see themselves as working with a higher power in order to confirm the justice of God on earth. The world's justice is of little consequence when God is on your side, according to the Klan. Protestantism is the way of God, and if you are not following the way of God then justice will not be available to you.

Criterion 6 is related to equality. In its very nature the Klan is set up in a way that is unequal. Ironically, the KKK has worked towards an internal structure that includes white, Protestant women's groups in order to have a more equal organization. They have also regulated their leadership structure so it is more transparent in relation to upward mobility within the organization. This is where equality stops. The KKK is theologically based on the idea that God has predestined some groups to be higher than others in relation to social status. This inequality is based on certain criteria, but one of those is tradition. There is no negotiation on being white, and there is no negotiation on being Protestant as requirements for being a part of the KKK. They have used tradition as a means by which they can create an unequal society, furthering the us versus them situation that they see as divinely ordained. They not only believe that they are racially, denominationally and geographically the best version of God-fearing Americans, but they also believe that those who do not fit their criteria do not deserve to be in power or to participate in activities that are gifted to Americans. For example, why should people of colour vote when they are not 'truly' Americans, according to the Klan? This group is based on the idea that inequality is not an evil system, it is just the way of the world. Also, when people who are outside the Klan community try to challenge instances of inequality, the Klan is there to re-establish God's ordained order. This is what we see in terms of the Klan of the reconstruction, the 1920s, the Civil Rights Movement, and indeed what we are seeing in 2022 and beyond with the Christian Identity movement.

Notes

1 A. N. Williams, 'Traditions' in *The Oxford Handbook of Systematic Theology*, ed. John Webster, Kathryn Tanner and Iain Torrance (Oxford: Oxford University Press, 2007), p. 363.

2 Williams, 'Traditions', p. 368.

3 Williams, 'Traditions', p. 366.

4 Tito Paredes, 'Ecclesiological Traditions and the Construction of Autochthonous Identities', *Journal of Latin American Theology* 12.1 (2018), p. 102.

5 Lausanne Covenant in Paredes, 'Ecclesiological Traditions', p. 103.

6 William J. Simmons quoted in Kelly J. Baker, 'Evangelizing Klansmen, Nationalizing the South: Faith, Fraternity, and Lost Cause Religion in the 1920s Klan', *Perspectives in Religious Studies* 39.3 (Fall 2012), p. 265.

7 Alex Fox, 'Nearly 2,000 Black Americans were Lynched during Reconstruction', *Smithsonian Magazine* (18 June 2020), https://www.smithsonianmag.com/smart-news/nearly-2000-black-americans-were-lynched-during-reconstruction-180975120/ (accessed 8.6.2022).

8 Simmons quoted in Baker, 'Evangelizing Klansmen', p. 261.

9 Kelly J. Baker, *The Gospel According to the Klan: The KKK's Appeal to Protestant America, 1915–1930* (Lawrence, KS: University of Kansas Press, 2011), p. 5.

10 Hiram Wesley Evans quoted in Juan O. Sanchez, *Religion and the Ku Klux Klan* (Jefferson, NC: McFarland Publishers, 2016), p. 33.

11 Baker, *The Gospel According to the Klan*, p. 10.

12 Baker, *The Gospel According to the Klan*, p. 14 (my italics).

13 Baker, *The Gospel According to the Klan*, p. 17.

14 Baker, *The Gospel According to the Klan*, p. 18.

15 Baker, *The Gospel According to the Klan*, p. 19.

16 Baker, *The Gospel According to the Klan*, p. 79.

17 The *Menace* in Baker, *The Gospel According to the Klan*, p. 175.

18 Simmons in Baker, *The Gospel According to the Klan*, p. 175.

19 Baker, *The Gospel According to the Klan*, p. 176.

20 John Blake, 'An "Imposter Christianity" is threatening American Democracy', *CNN* (24 July 2022), https://www.cnn.com/2022/07/24/us/white-christian-nationalism-blake-cec/index.html (accessed 15.8.2022).

21 Philip Gorski quoted in Blake, 'An "Imposter Christianity"'.

22 Blake, 'An "Imposter Christianity"'.

23 Doctrinal Statement of Beliefs quoted in Sanchez, *Religion and the Ku Klux Klan*, p. 180.

24 Doctrinal Statement of Beliefs quoted in Sanchez, *Religion and the Ku Klux Klan*, p. 180.

25 Doctrinal Statement of Beliefs quoted in Sanchez, *Religion and the Ku Klux Klan*, p. 180.

26 Kelly J. Baker quoted in Sanchez, *Religion and the Ku Klux Klan*, p. 42.

27 Doctrinal Statement of Beliefs quoted in Sanchez, *Religion and the Ku Klux Klan*, p. 180.

28 Doctrinal Statement of Beliefs quoted in Sanchez, *Religion and the Ku Klux Klan*, p. 180.

7

The Massacre at Jonestown: A Bad Theology of Eschatology

Much like providence was a construct to understand the way that God worked in the world (or didn't work in the world), eschatology similarly offers a means by which humans can continue to flourish in a world that can be chaotic and uncertain. Eschatology is a study of the end times, at its very basic meaning, and it caters to the human need for 'meaning and hope in the face of finitude – both personal and cosmic'.[1] According to Anna Case-Winters, eschatology is important as it helps people to answer questions about the meaning and purpose of life, and to that end it encourages human flourishing and 'engenders a hope and a zest for life'.[2]

At its very core, eschatology deals with end times. That could be a personal or a cosmic end time. The cosmic end times are directly related to personal end times, however. Theology is not alone in contemplating the cosmic end times. Most scientists agree that there is a definitive and inevitable end of the earth as we know it. Personal end times are generally accepted as the finale of the state of being human – that is, death. Personal eschatology also deals with what happens after one dies, and also what happens to individual humans when the cosmic end times come to pass. According to Hans Schwarz: 'In its broadest sense the term "eschatology" includes all concepts of life beyond death and everything connected with it such as heaven and hell, paradise and immortality, resurrection and transmigration of the soul, rebirth and re-incarnation, and last judgment and doomsday.'[3]

In the Christian tradition, the Old Testament texts do have themes of the end times. They are divided into three distinct areas: the destiny of humanity (Israel specifically), the last judgement and the hope for a coming Messiah. First, despite being surrounded by religions in Egypt and Mesopotamia, the Israelites were not influenced by these cultures' obsession with the afterlife. As a result, they were very focused on the here and now when it came to individual eschatology. While the Egyptians went to great lengths to prepare their dead for the long journey to the afterlife, the Israelites did not think much about what happened once you left this world. They believed, of course, that God would take care of them after their earthly life, but what that life looked like was not clear. Schwarz states:

> The Israelites did not waste much thought on a life beyond. Of course, they knew that death was not the end of human existence, but they did not understand it as the transition to a better hereafter or to a netherworldly torture chamber. It was at best a shadowy existence that they envisioned.[4]

Death was something that was brought upon the world by the rebellion in Genesis, and while God was in charge of both life and death, this was in a merciful way. One of the greatest blessings in the Old Testament was for a leader to live a long life, for this showed that God approved of their work on earth. Any notion of a last judgement or end times in a cosmic sense was therefore orchestrated by God and God alone. In early writings, the Israelites saw God's judgement on earth, as they travelled to the Promised Land and beyond. Later prophets developed a more robust view of end times, a Day of the Lord, that would wipe the slate clean of creation in a devastating way. Salvation becomes a theme among the prophets as well. Whether it is salvation or destruction it is firmly in the hands of God as to what will come to pass. However, if a nation is to survive they must follow the laws and ways of God in order to flourish. It is in this time of prophecy and discussions of salvation that we begin to see mention of a suffering servant or a Messiah who is to come to earth as an advocate. The apocalyptic prophets adjusted this understanding of the Messiah slightly to be one who would defend Israel and act as an extension of God:

> God is the Lord of the whole earth; Judaism is the embodiment of religion for all humanity; and Israel is the instrument for the establishment of God's worldwide rule. From their vantage point, the apocalyptists assumed they could see the past, present, and future in one continuous progression preordained by God.[5]

It should be noted that there is clear influence on the Jewish understanding of the afterlife when they are exiled and come into contact with the Zoroastrianism religion with its emphasis on the end times. Suddenly the shadowy and vague land of the Jewish afterlife had actual forms and specifics. There was a need to purify those who acted against God in order to get them ready for these end times. There was a good and a bad place. Those of the Christian tradition will probably recognize these themes, as they are key influencers in the New Testament.

In the New Testament the end times are more at the forefront and centre of the story. The figure of Jesus is the centre of the text in the New Testament, and he comes from a Jewish background. While one cannot deny the influence of the Jewish tradition on Jesus, and his views of the end times, it is important to see these two sections of text (Old and New Testaments) as being distinct in their traditional history. That being said, Jesus did have ideas about the end times that he proclaims from the very beginning of his ministry. The word that could summarize Jesus' view of the coming end times is 'immediacy': 'Jesus did not give listeners a timetable and inform them in detail about things that were going to happen at some future point, but he addressed his audience in such a way that an immediate decision was implied.'[6]

Jesus did not mince words about the end times, or the coming kingdom. According to Jesus, the kingdom of God was happening on earth at the very moment of his appearance. This is why immediate decisions had to be made; personal and cosmic eschatology was at hand. The kingdom of God had been realized through Jesus, and there were aspects of the kingdom that would be coming in the future. Jesus was extremely hesitant, however, about setting any firm dates or times for this realization. He said that no one knew that except for God. According to Schwarz: 'This refusal to set any dates which would enable humans to prepare for the impending end shows that setting such a date is a divine prerogative. The kingdom of God is not to be realized by humans; they have no way of speeding it up or determining who gets the seats of honor.'[7]

While Jesus did not predict the last days, as only God could do that, he strongly emphasized the importance of getting oneself prepared and aligned with God for the coming full realization of the kingdom of God on earth. Jesus saw himself as 'the final self-disclosure of God'.[8] Choosing to follow Jesus would mean that when people died, they would be judged as loyal to God's kingdom, and as a result they would be granted eternal life. This could hint at the immediate nature of Jesus' message. Because no one knew the date or time of God's full realization of the kingdom on earth, everyone had to be prepared. When Jesus was captured and ultimately killed and resurrected, there were theological questions about this coming full realization of the kingdom. Many of the disciples saw Jesus as the one who was going to save Israel in the here and now. With his death, this idea of what Jesus was actually teaching about the end times came into question.

To avoid what some saw as a contradiction between Jesus' message of the impending realization of the kingdom of God on earth and his death on the cross, we see authors of the New Testament emphasize the importance of the early church. According to St Paul, the church is where the faithful should remain until the impending end of days. The interim between now and those end times gives Christians the time to prepare themselves for the full realization of the kingdom of God on earth. It is also a time to tell others about the message of Jesus and to bring them into the Christian church. The eschatology for the early church meant that God would return to earth to be in 'communion'[9] with God's people: 'God will overcome the resistance of all ungodly people and powers. This salvational confidence that God will be victorious over everybody and everything gave the Christian community the strength to survive as a small and quite often persecuted group.'[10]

The book of Revelation clearly added to the conversation. I say 'added' because the idea that Revelation cleared up any questions related to eschatology and the end times is ridiculous, based solely on the sheer number of interpretations that come from that text. However, we do get certain phrases and ideas from the book that have been constructed into a variety of eschatological theories that will prove important to this conversation. First, we have the idea of a time period in human history referred to as the great tribulation (mentioned in Matthew by Jesus but solidified in translations of Revelation). There will be wars, plagues, disease, lack of food and resources, as well as false prophets who try to persuade the followers of Jesus to turn against him. Another common theme solidified in the book of Revelation is the idea of millennialism in various forms. This is the belief that there will be a time period of a thousand years when there is a peaceful reign of Jesus on earth.

Once the early church fathers and theologians got hold of concepts like the millennial reign, final judgement and the great tribulation, there were a series of interpretations that began to emerge. The belief in what will actually happen depends greatly on what religious group or denomination one finds oneself in, but it is worth mentioning some of the conclusions that have emerged throughout church history about the end times. These generally have been summarized into four main theories: post-tribulational pre-millennialism; pre-tribulational (dispensational) pre-millennialism; postmillennialism; and amillennialism. Pre-millennialism refers to a belief that in the end times Jesus will return to earth, and following this return there will be a thousand-year peaceful period that will conclude with the final judgement. There are two versions of this particular belief. One version says that those who are Christian will have to go through the great tribulation before Jesus' return, and the other says that there will be a rapture of Christian people away from the earth prior to the great tribulation. Post-millennialism postulates that there will be a one-thousand-year reign and then the last judgement. Finally, amillennialism says that the one-thousand-year reign is symbolic and not actually one thousand years, and that we are currently living in that symbolic time period now. After the symbolic one-thousand-year reign there will be a final judgement.

Because of the ambiguity in the Christian text about the end times there are multiple theories about how it will all come to pass. While this could be seen as an exercise in creativity about the theological implications of the end times, what we have seen is that it has in fact bred a very particular form of bad theology. People are concerned about their own personal end as well as the end of the world. As a result of this concern (which can look like paranoia or fear at times), a vulnerability exists whereby people may be drawn into groups that claim to have a much firmer understanding of how it will all take place at the end. Death is something that no human can escape, and as a result there is an urgency in the desire for some to know what happens at the end (that is, the end of their lives and the end of the earth period). Those who claim to have answers are in a very powerful position, and that power can lend itself to the exploitation of people's fears and worries about the end times.

A religious history of cults in the USA

Before we get to our discussion of the snapshot of this chapter, Jonestown, I want to go through a little bit of the history of doomsday cults in the context of the USA. This is to give further brief examples of the way that the theology of eschatology has been manipulated in order to gain control over a group of people in a variety of contexts. The reason I have chosen the USA as a case study specifically is because the religious history of the USA is completely inundated with doomsday cults and end-of-the-world groups. It is almost as if the history of religion in the USA is a history of eschatology. In reference to the USA, the scholar Charles Ferguson wrote: 'It should be obvious to any man who is not one himself that the land [USA] is overrun with messiahs.'[11]

Professor Phillip Jenkins has spent a great deal of research time on the area of cults in the USA, and has developed definitive characteristics of these groups. He offers the following:

> In common parlance, cults are exotic religions that practice spiritual totalitarianism: members owe fanatical obedience to the group and to its charismatic leaders, who enforce their authority through mind-control techniques or brainwashing. According to the stereotype, cult members live separated from the 'normal' world, sometimes socially, in the sense of being cut off from previous friends and family, and sometimes also spatially, in a special residence house or a remote compound. Other cult characteristics include financial malpractice and deceit by the group or its leaders, the exploitation of members, and sexual unorthodoxy.[12]

Jenkins wrestles with the idea that cults are far more prevalent in the USA than in other countries. According to Jenkins, the focus on the end times has never been far from the centre of American religious life. This is because the freedom of religion that settlers were looking for in the colonies gave a much freer range when it comes to how one 'does religion'. According to Jenkins: 'In its earliest days colonial New England was a refuge for those seeking to live godly lives uncontaminated by the sinful world, very much the same motivation that today drives believers into remote enclaves.'[13] Although most of the first sociologically defined cults in the USA were branches of Christianity, there were also various other cults that came together under the banner of theosophy, spiritualism, masonry, pseudoscience and sexual/drug liberation and so on. (or a combination of various areas into one group).

Although we can historically map these groups coming together from the very beginning of the colonies, there are periods of US history that seem to get more attention than others with regard to cult panic. Does this mean that there were more cults around at that particular time than others? Probably not, but Jenkins defines these time periods as those when people became increasingly concerned about the threat of cults, but not necessarily their numerical existence. He associates these time periods of cult awareness with population increases. Logically, this makes sense. If there are more young people in the world, there is an increase in the possibility of those young people joining organizations. For example, there was a population increase from 1890 to 1915, as well as the post-Second World War baby boom. These are time periods when there was a high level of suspicion around cults and sects in the USA.

Alongside increased population, other factors can lead to cult panic. Racial, gender and sexual social changes that challenge the status quo can also result in the general population becoming concerned. Certain swathes of the population, specifically those who have been discriminated against, begin to look for alternatives to the prevailing systems. Among those systems is the religious status quo. According to Jenkins: 'New religions flourish by providing believers with what they cannot obtain in the mainstream organizations of the day: sects and cults live on the unpaid bills of the churches.'[14]

As an aside, it should be noted that even sociologically the word 'cult' has been attributed to most established religious traditions/denominations at some stage, even the 'legitimate' traditions in the world. Cult is often associated with new religious movements, and the truth of the matter is that all traditions were new at some point. Some survive and thrive past the cult stage, and others do not, but it is worth noting that in some of these peak panic periods concerning cults the panicking was over religious traditions that are now considered mainstream.

One of the main periods when the cult panic was very real and widespread was the 1960s in the USA. The children of the Second World War generation were not like their parents. They were not going to adhere to church every Sunday, 2.5 kids and microwave dinners. They were exploring areas of drugs, sexuality, music, race relations and beyond. The 'beyond' in that sentence also included religion, and new religious movements (and old movements from Asia that were viewed as 'new') became increasingly popular as young people searched for something outside of their traditional Christian upbringing to offer meaning. This led to a rise in anti-cult movements from concerned parents and groups who were worried about what they perceived as an increasing threat to their way of life and their 'religious normality'.[15] In the seventeenth century, cults were seen as using witchcraft to gain followers. In the nineteenth century this evolved to become hypnotism, and finally in the twentieth century it was framed as brainwashing and mind control. As a result, the anti-cult groups focused on what they described as intervention and de-programming of the mind control over their loved ones. The groups began to formalize, and in the 1970s you had the Citizens Freedom Foundation. By the 1980s, you had the Cult Awareness Network, and in 1979 the American Family Foundation was created in order to help people who had formerly been in cults. What event could have led to this kind of reaction to new religions in the USA in the 1960s and 1970s? According to Rabbi Maurice Davis: 'The path of the cults leads to Jonestown.'[16] And it is this snapshot that we further explore as a bad theology of eschatology.

Jonestown

James Warren 'Jim' Jones was born in a small town in Indiana in 1931. Growing up in this small town meant that Jim attended a wide variety of Pentecostal churches that were prevalent in the area at the time. As a child, Jim would often play pranks on local churches that he viewed as not living up to the Christian name, a great foretelling of what was to come.[17] In 1949, Jim married and consequently moved to Indianapolis with his new wife. The city was a hotbed of racial discrimination, and this was said to have fuelled Jim's desire to pursue racial equality in the world.

Jones worked as a student pastor at Somerset Methodist Church, Indiana, where he impressed congregants with his preaching and prophecy as well as his healing abilities. His views on controversial areas such as racial equality and socialism, however, caused some disconnect from his congregants, and by 1953 he had branched out to start his own church, Community Unity Church. His church was composed largely of people of colour, and they were amazed by his steadfast message of racial equality. Jones attracted large crowds at his congregation, mostly as a result of the miraculous faith healing that took place there. He and his wife also began to grow their family by adopting children of different racial backgrounds.

By the 1960s, Jones's newly named church, the People's Temple, had become officially affiliated with the Christian denomination The Christian Church (Disciples of Christ), and Jones consequently was ordained in the denomination in 1964. By 1965, Jones had developed a fear of nuclear war and decided to move his church to Ukiah in California. As his congregation grew, he opened up two different sites for his church, one in San Francisco and one in Los Angeles. In 1974, the newspaper *The Sacramento Bee* said the People's Temple appeared to be the largest Protestant church in northern California. The attendance at this time was estimated to be between 3,000 and 20,000 people at Sunday services.

As Jones's popularity continued to gain momentum, so did the scrutiny of some of his practices. By the 1970s, the People's Temple was being heavily criticized for various offences such as mishandling donations, physical abuse and mistreating children. Jones became increasingly paranoid about being held accountable in the USA for these infractions. Having previously visited the South American country of Guyana, he decided he wanted to establish a jungle compound that would be a utopia for his followers. The congregation moved to the homestead of Jonestown in Guyana in 1977; Jones referred to this compound as being the 'Promised Land' for his congregation. A safe haven where his followers could realize the dreams of communal living that Jones had dreamt of.

Just before the great move to Guyana, the allegations increased exponentially against Jones. Along with financial misappropriation and violence in the community, there were also several publications in the local San Francisco area that were looking to expose Jones's misdeeds and show the People's Temple for what it was – a cult. In 1977, immediately before the move, *New West* magazine published a tell-all about Jones and the People's Temple. The information from the magazine was based on stories given to the publication from defectors. Jones did not want the publication to come out and tried to block it completely, but he was unsuccessful. Unfortunately, at this stage it was too late. By the time Jones left for Guyana there were 70 people living in the compound full time, and by the end of the year there were 900 people living there. The demographics of the People's Temple in Guyana at this time were '75% black, 20% white, and 5% Hispanic, Asian or Native Americans; two thirds were women; 300 were minors; and 150 were over the age of sixty-five'.[18]

It wasn't long before the members of the People's Temple began to realize that the land that had been set aside for the People's Temple in Guyana was by no means a paradise or a Promised Land. The members of the Temple worked hard in the unforgiving territory of the jungle in order to survive. They were punished for going against authority. They did not have the option to visit the USA and their passports were taken from them in order to ensure that they would not be able to leave the jungle. The group also had to go through several 'white night' drills that were enacted in order to test loyalty among members of the People's Temple. These drills corresponded with perceived attacks on the community and were led by Jones. The threat of the poisoned juice was present in one of these white nights – only to be proven to be just a drill after people were not killed.

One of the key aspects of power that Jones wielded over his community was its isolation from the People's Temple's friends and family. They were completely under his control out in the jungle, and he had set up the community in such isolation that they would have little opportunity to just walk away from the group. By 1978, a number of concerned friends and family were filing lawsuits against Jim Jones. This group, known as the Concerned Relatives, rallied to the state of California to reach out to their loved ones on their behalf. In November 1978, Congressman Leo Ryan ventured to Guyana in order to investigate Jonestown. Ryan was relatively impressed with Jonestown based on what he experienced and saw. There were people who wanted to leave, but overwhelmingly the community was steadfast in their mission and their place at the People's Temple. He confirmed to Jones that he would write a positive report about his experiences at Jonestown, and he would take those who wanted to return home with him back to the USA. What Ryan did not know was that Jones was not going to accept defectors. Jones clearly would accept no disobedience amid his increasing paranoia (at this stage his mental illness and drug abuse had caused some members to be deeply concerned). Jones sent members of the community to the airstrip where congressman Ryan, members of the media and the defectors were about to take off. They shot and killed Ryan and four of the members of the party. As the assassins returned to Jonestown, it became clear to Jones that this was the last of the white nights, and that he had run out of options for the community to continue to live.

Around 6 p.m., Jones began the final white night whereby he gave his followers, around 900 in number, a lethal dose of cyanide, tranquillizers and fruit juice. Members of all ages who did not defect, escape or play dead were killed. Men, women and children were included in this group. Jones, ever the narcissist, recorded this final white night. In this last tape,

Jones claims that he wanted 'to give you the good life ... in spite of all I've tried a handful of our people with a lie have made our lives impossible'.[19] He talks extensively on this tape about how they had tried to attempt something that the world was not ready for. Their experiment of living together in a communal way that didn't recognize race or class or other aspects that put people in boxes was revolutionary. 'I'm the best friend you'll ever have', Jones assures his congregation. And also, 'Without me life has no meaning.'[20]

Jones went on to tell his congregation that despite their attempts at this utopian society they had been betrayed by defectors, by the organization Concerned Relatives and even by the US government itself. He convinced his followers that because of what happened with Leo Ryan the People's Temple was under immediate attack, including the children in the compound. He says: 'So my opinion is that we be kind to seniors and take the potion like they used to take in ancient Greece, and step over quietly. We are not committing suicide – it's a revolutionary act. We can't go back ... There is no way we can survive.'[21] According to Jones, there is no way that they can survive as things are. There are dissenters among his congregation who say that there are possibilities other than suicide, but Jones deflects these responses. To one dissenter Jones says: 'I'm not speaking as an administrator here, I'm talking as a prophet ... You'll regret this very day if you don't die ... The best testimony we can have is to leave this god damn world.'[22]

Instead of seeing the act as one of mass suicide, Jones tells his congregation that they are instead choosing to lay down their lives rather than be killed by outsiders. When hysteria around the children's reaction to the poison is clearly increasing on the tape, Jones says: 'The way the children are laying there now. I'd rather see them lay like that than see them have to die like the Jews did.'[23] The last words on the tape before all goes silent is Jones saying: 'We didn't commit suicide, we committed a revolutionary act of suicide.'[24] By the end of the night, 900 people were dead, including Jim Jones.

A bad theology of eschatology

Although Jones had a fraught relationship with the label, in effect, the Peoples Temple was Christian ... and officially remained a recognized Disciples of Christ church, and Jones an ordained minister, until its implosion.[25]

Phoebe Duke-Mosier does an excellent job in her article 'Drinking the Kool-Aid: Discourses of Death at Jonestown' of showing how religion is often portrayed as being irrelevant to such horrible atrocities. I have previously discussed the idea that in rhetoric about religion there is an inclination to consider something non-religious if it is not seen as doing something that is good. In this book I have tried to continue the narrative that just because something presents as bad or good does not mean that it is any more or less 'religion' or 'theology'. There is bad religion and there is bad theology. Duke-Mosier takes this idea and goes into detail as to how the Jonestown massacre was presented in the media.

In her article, Duke-Mosier explains that the media tried to present Jonestown as a 'cult menace hegemony'.[26] By using the word 'hegemony' it furthered the idea that the group at Jonestown was dominated by a force so great that it could not control what would happen next. She also states: 'Jones and his followers continue to be described in derogatory or pathological terms: Jones was a "madman," the People's Temple was "cult"; those who died were "brainwashed".'[27] Duke-Mosier thinks that this was a discourse tool that was used in order to make Jonestown seem like the ultimate 'other', and to further prove that there was no understanding as to why the members of the People's Temple did what they did.

There is the 'unreligionification'[28] of Jonestown, as Duke-Mosier puts it. The members of the People's Temple were described as 'frauds, hypocrites, or dupes ... (i.e., being bad, they can't really be religious)'.[29] This unreligionification will have been comforting to people who read the story about Jonestown, as they believed that this could never happen to 'good' Christians. My argument, and indeed Duke-Mosier's argument, is that they actually were being religious, and they were enacting their own theological beliefs up until the end.

What was the fundamental bad theological belief that caused those in the People's Temple to ultimately end their own lives? The phrase Jones uses, 'revolutionary suicide', was not one that he made up himself. It was used by the Black Panther Minister of Defense, Huey Newton, in his book *Revolutionary Suicide*. Jones was drawn to this phrase because it admitted that all life had an end date, but that one could choose to use one's death in a way that would make for change in an oppressive world. According to David Chidester: 'Revolutionary suicide embraced the certainty of death in the militant struggle for liberation against the overwhelming forces of oppression.'[30] Newton, of course, disowned the use of revolutionary suicide by the People's Temple. This in no way stopped revolutionary suicide becoming a seemingly inevitable ending for the congregation even from the beginning of its creation. It was also a central focus of their particular eschatology, as it gave a purpose to their continued cause of pushing against racism and oppression of all kinds: 'Revolutionary suicide was a strategy designed to symbolically invert the dehumanizing subclassifications of oppression, racism, and poverty by claiming eternal, superhuman immortality through revolutionary action.'[31]

To put together a coherent theology of Jones and the People's Temple is difficult. Jones had what could only be described as an evolutionary theology. This is quite common in people who claim to know the end of the world is coming, as you have to adjust to the continued fact that the world has not yet come to an end. Jones found that latching on to the idea that his community was continuously being targeted, continuously being oppressed by the outside world (especially the USA and capitalism), was a way to prove the end was coming. He quotes Marx when it suits him, and then later he will quote Jesus. He was able to patchwork various theological ideas to suit himself throughout his career, but one thing that remained steadfast was this idea of oppression and ultimately escaping oppression. When analysed deeper this looks very much as if Jones believed himself to be living in some sort of great tribulation theological reality, and as 'Dad' he was called to protect his community from this continued oppression.

What we can see about Jones's theology is that he would focus on a theme or an action and then use the biblical text to 'proof text' or prove that his idea was correct based on biblical references. For example, his obsession with revolutionary suicide led him to invoke Christian texts like John 10.18 and 1 Corinthians 13.3 to justify his beliefs. Jones is quoted as saying:

> That's what Jesus said, 'No man, no man, no man shall take my life. I will lay it down.' That's what he said. He meant he'd lay it down when he got ready. Some of these Christians don't understand this. We're more Christian than they ever could be. Paul said, 'It's alright, give your body to be burned, but be sure you've got charity, which means Principle.' What is pure love? Communism! So in other words, Paul was saying, 'Give your body to be burned, set it afire of necessity to get a revolutionary message [across], but be sure you've got communism in your heart.' Right? That's what would be charity today. [You] can't have charity without communism. So this is nothing new – giving your body, going out and committing suicide, taking a few enemies with you.[32]

In the above quote, we can see a hodgepodge of theological interpretation, biblical texts, communist rhetoric and discussions of suicide. All of it is mashed together in order to put forth Jones's main message of communism and suicide, all through the lens of the justification of the biblical text. Jones is doing theology in this sense. He is interpreting the text and using it as a means of justifying his own bad behaviour and actions. There is also a sense here of superiority. He tells his congregation that through revolutionary suicide you won't just be Christians, but you'll be the best kind of Christians. He goes on to say that the world had the message of Jesus and Paul wrong, but Jones was there to lead his people to the right interpretation. This right interpretation, according to Jones, was based on ideas of communism, tribulation and oppression, and the release of suicide. It would not have been hard, therefore, to convince the People's Temple that the intruders from the USA were not there to help them, but had found a way of continuing to oppress them; that the oppressors were there to take them away from the community that was helping to enlighten them, and back to capitalist USA, where Jones says they would all get brainwashed back to what they were before.

Jones references the Greek tradition, where the action of revolutionary suicide was commonplace. In ancient times it was seen as a release from a society that had ceased to be liveable for an individual. Taking control of one's own death showcased a means of agency that no oppressive forces could take. While there was no clear indication in Jones's world of heaven and hell at the end, there was an idea of immortality in the face of laying down one's life in the midst of tribulation. The idea of revolutionary suicide as a means of salvation is present in the theology of the People's Temple: 'At Jonestown, collective suicide came to be regarded as a route to salvation.'[33] Could someone arguably be a part of the world and its great tribulation and still reach salvation? By all accounts the answer is yes, but you would have to live in a world full of hate and oppression. Jones believed he was offering an alternative to that. Unfortunately for all, according to Jones, the oppressive forces had found them. As a result, Jones implores his followers to see that this cycle of oppression, escape and oppression again will continue to follow them. To Jones, it was better to purposefully stop the cycle now in order to save them from the hell that was on earth. And there was no better person to lead them out of this land of oppression than Jones. He saw the God of the Christian text as imaginary. Accordingly, Jones saw himself as being the real God on earth. He also saw the Christian text as being created by white men in order to maintain power throughout history.

Criterion 1 for bad theology involves human flourishing. What is interesting about the story of Jonestown is that, by all accounts, the beginning of this group was intended to work towards human flourishing. In the context of an oppressive society, Jones claimed to be working towards uniting different communities and creating a more equal society. However, what eventually transpired in Guyana was clearly not related to human flourishing. Until the very end, Jones claimed that he was trying to build the best of worlds for the people of his congregation, but this was clearly not true. Even in California, he was accused of abuses, both with money and people. When the group got to Guyana, he was so intent on getting this perfect society going that he put his members to forced labour to set up the compound. By most accounts, this was labour in which Jones himself did not actively participate.

I believe strongly that Jonestown wouldn't have existed at all if Jim Jones had not started his work with the People's Temple under the banner of human flourishing. There is the question of whether Jones himself thought he was creating a world of human flourishing, even with the abuses in the USA and Guyana. I believe he did, which is why he had no doubts whatsoever about what he was doing. When you read his texts and his sermons it's clear that Jones strongly believed what he was saying. He became so intoxicated with the idea of leading his congregation to social equality and human flourishing that he himself became the thing that prevented human flourishing. There are strong (self-proclaimed) Messiah complexes present here, and at some point Jones' message of human flourishing became so overwhelming that he destroyed those he was hoping to lead to flourishing. By the end of the last white night, people pointed this out, but Jones had already taken his followers too far to turn back.

For criterion 2 there is a need to go back to Jones's Messiah-like complex. He became so overwhelmed by his message of communism and equality that it consumed him. Anyone who tried to challenge him was discredited and ignored. At one stage, in that final tape, a dissenter in the group challenges

Jones and says: 'As long as there is life there is hope.'[34] Jones fires back immediately, saying: 'At some place that hope runs out 'cos everybody dies ... I'd like to choose my own kinda death for a change ... I'm tired of being tormented to hell.'[35] His lack of reflection in these interactions, even at the end, shows how much Jones believed himself to be an actual God among these people. In the tape transcripts of the last white night, his own wife is heard begging him not to follow through with the poisoning, but she is also ignored. No one is able to get to him at this stage to be able to garner any kind of reflection on this action. Jones is convinced that this is the only way, and he is not willing to accept people breaking ranks.

This is not uncommon among those deemed as doomsday leaders. It often feels as though any type of reflection would show a kind of weakness on their part. They have to be so utterly right about their eschatological beliefs and hold to those beliefs no matter what. Jones did evolve his theological understandings throughout his career, but he held fast to this idea of the tribulation that was around them, and the need for revolutionary suicide if that tribulation got to be too much. The rest, quite honestly, was theological fluff that could be adapted to a given time or place. So while Jones might change his mind on some things in order to maintain power, he did not change his mind on things related to the end times. And this is shown clearly in the end result of the People's Temple. The congregation is mostly in favour of his ideas of revolutionary suicide, but he does not even take one second to consider the dissenters. The decision in his mind has been made, and because he is 'Dad,' as they called him, the decision is not to be reflected upon.

It is with criterion 3 that Jones really built his entire community. Most cult leaders create this kind of us versus them environment. If these leaders can move people away from their friends and family (who are not in the group) then they can have more solid control over said people. This is exclusively because they can then be the ultimate authority in a person's life. If there is no feedback, criticism or reflection from anyone in the 'outside' world, then the word of the leader is the final say. This is ideal for anyone who is trying to get total and complete control over a person or peoples. There is a difficulty, however, in getting people away from those they love, for obvious reasons. A leader in these kinds of groups has to create a dualism whereby the person in the cult must choose what life they are going to live: the life of the leader or the life with their friends and family.

It isn't just about choice of lifestyle, however, it is a choice between good and evil, life and death, good and bad, right and wrong and so on. The consequences of not choosing the cult leader have to be quite severe. This is not just choosing to live in another country in order to follow a religious tradition; this has to be escaping persecution at the highest level. It has to be living out the real meaning of what your version of God intended for the world. And there also have to be elements of the fact that those outside of the community are a part of your oppression, that they are somehow the ones who are causing the negativity in the world, and that interacting with them would cause you not to fulfil that which you want to achieve in the world (and what God intended that people should achieve). In Scientology those who are outside of the religious community are declared 'suppressive', and that sums up perfectly this idea of the us versus them mentality in some of these groups.

There has been, and will always be, a form of us versus them in any religious tradition. This is the nature of being a part of any group, but the us versus them in the snapshot of Jonestown shows a different version of this type of sectioning-off from society. Jones was able to convince his entire community that everyone in the USA was out to get them, even the government itself. He was so proficient in creating this us versus them mentality that he was able to move a group of 900-plus people away from their entire lives in the USA to a compound in the jungle in South America. This was under the banner that they were going to build a utopian society (us) outside of a world that was constantly trying to tear that utopia apart in the USA (them). Anyone who is in that outside world is a part of the oppression that created the need to move in order to realize their utopia. When the organization Concerned Relatives and Congressman Ryan came to check on Jonestown, in a way they were playing into Jones's game. He made it seem as though they weren't concerned families or representatives, but were the oppression of the old world that had found them. The 'them' was still trying to make sure they were unable to accomplish what they desired in Guyana. The 'oppressive them' was not going to let them exist in peace. Jones passed this narrative on intensely and, while some defectors saw through it, the majority of his followers saw the vision that he was perpetuating.

There would have been no final white night at Jonestown without an us versus them mentality. Jones made it absolutely clear that the USA was out to get them and their children, and that there was no other way to escape the torment of the old world. The 'oppressive them' wanted to return them all to the USA and brainwash them back into the complacency of the world they once knew. Jones pleaded with his congregation not to go back to such a world, and not to let the 'oppressive them' come and return children to the old ways.

Criterion 4 really ties directly into criterion 3. It discusses the idea that your theology and tradition are isolated from the rest of the world or from other traditions/theology. While we have spoken about physical isolation in this section, it is also important to speak about the isolation that Jones had theologically. Jones was a Disciples of Christ minister and, full disclosure, so am I, but he manipulated and evolved his theology into something that would fit the world view that he wanted to create. He started in a tradition where he was doing great works (at face value) in the world of equality and equity. He had views on the end of the world, on oppression and tribulation, and ideas about the way that his congregation should live in order to have their best life. As the years passed, however, he moved further away from any sort of recognizable Christian tradition. He knew his followers had started off in that tradition, so he kept some of the ideas that he began with.

But soon ideas of God were replaced by Jones himself. Ideas of the great tribulation were replaced with racism and sexism and the USA itself. Understandings of the end times and the return of God's kingdom was replaced by creating the kingdom of God on earth.

So while you could definitely argue that Jones was isolated physically from the rest of the world, what we also see is that he had isolated his theology and the theological understandings of his congregation from the rest of the tradition. This isolation meant that there was no challenging from denominational bodies or from other churches or ministers in the tradition. And when Jones finally moved his congregation to Guyana, that isolation was complete. There were no Disciples of Christ congregations in that region to challenge his conclusions, or really any similar Protestant denominations at all. He was traditionally and theologically isolated to continue to evolve and manipulate the message to his own ends.

Criterion 5 is related to justice in the wider world. Jones would have been outraged to find anyone who did not see his theological understandings as being centred on justice. He believed that he was creating a socialist utopia that flew in the face of everything that the USA stood for and encouraged. Justice was the cornerstone of his initial ministry. He believed the People's Temple could right the wrongs of the injustice of the society around him, and that they could show people a different way of living that did not centre on ideas like racism and sexism specifically (he had some ideas on sexuality, but let's just say they didn't lend themselves to justice). What we can see from the beginning is that the message of justice that Jones was preaching did not match with his actions. Accusations of abuses, both physical and financial, were reported from the start of his ministry. When the group moved to Guyana, there were injustices that occurred along the lines of work and labour distributions. Jones became increasingly erratic in his views of the congregation and his relation to them, especially in relation to his ownership of the women of the group. And finally, there was no justice on that last white night. There were many claims by Jones that the People's Temple was showing people how to live justly, and how to live together in harmony. But much like everything else that came out of Jones's mouth, the hypothetical theology did not relate to the actions and the Practical Theology of what was actually taking place on the ground. There was no justice on that day in November 1978.

Finally, criterion 6 focuses on the desire for equality in the wider world. Much like everything else that has been discussed, we can reference the fact that in the beginning Jones said that he wanted to live in a more equal society, and that he was tired of the injustice and inequality in the USA. The more we dig we can see that there was nothing equal about a personality like his leading a community. Fundamentally, he wanted to present himself as someone who was just like the rest of his congregation. At the last white night, he states in one breath: 'I'm not speaking as an administrator here. I'm speaking as a prophet.' And then in the next breath: 'I can't separate myself from the pain of my people.'[36] Jones had the desire for his church to see him as their equal, and for everyone to be equal in his congregation. This was not the case. Jones was forever dictating what should be done at the People's Temple, both in the USA and in Guyana. He did not ask for discussion, but instead declared himself a prophet and God on earth. Therefore, while he continued to spout about the message of equality, he was creating a society that was completely top down. He even had a circle of advisers he trusted more than others. They became watchdogs for everyone else in the group. Their main jobs were to spot dissenters and people who were trying to go against Jones. This hardly speaks to an equal, utopian, socialist society.

At the very end, Jones proved once and for all just how unequal the society actually was. He declared that they all must die. They must die for reasons he appeared to make up as he went along. These reasons superficially seemed to be based on the fact that Jones's ego couldn't handle anyone actually leaving his congregation. As a result, he felt he had to punish them and anyone who was with them. Hardly equal. The declaration of the need for death was met with minimal dissent, but there *were* dissenters there. They were dismissed outright and barely given any time to speak. The people around them yelled loudly and cheered for Jones. This is the illusion of democracy at its finest. While the dissenters and supporters may have felt that they had an equal voice in this decision-making process, they did not. With one hand Jones offered a microphone for voices to discuss, and with the other hand he armed guards to kill anyone who didn't agree with his decision. Seeing the bodies lying on the ground in Jonestown is a startling image. In Jones's mind, I believe he had a vision that someone would arrive and find them in this state and see how utopian and equal their society was. When the world gazed upon the scene, all they saw was horror. This was not some equal society where decisions were shared. No, this was a death scene dictated by an egotistical, doomsday preacher, with a basic armchair theology he bent to his every will.

Notes

1 Anna Case-Winters, 'The End? Christian Eschatology and the End of the World', *Interpretation: a Journal of Bible and Theology* 70.1 (2016), p. 62.

2 Case-Winters, 'The End?', p. 63.

3 Hans Schwarz, *Eschatology* (Grand Rapids, MI: William B. Eerdmans, 2000), p. 26.

4 Schwarz, *Eschatology*, p. 36.

5 Schwarz, *Eschatology*, p. 53.

6 Schwarz, *Eschatology*, p. 69.

7 Schwarz, *Eschatology*, p. 71.

8 Schwarz, *Eschatology*, p. 75.

9 Schwarz, *Eschatology*, p. 98.

10 Schwarz, *Eschatology*, p. 98.

11 Charles Ferguson in Phillip Jenkins, *Mystics and Messiahs: Cults and New Religions in American History* (Oxford: Oxford University Press, 2000), p. 3.

12 Jenkins, *Mystics and Messiahs*, p. 4.

13 Jenkins, *Mystics and Messiahs*, p. 6.

14 Jenkins, *Mystics and Messiahs*, p. 21.

15 Jenkins, *Mystics and Messiahs*, p. 188.

16 Rabbi Maurice David in Jenkins, *Mystics and Messiah*, p. 187.

17 Phoebe Duke-Mosier, 'Drinking the Kool-Aid: Discourses of Death at Jonestown', *The Journal of Theta Alpha Kappa* (Fall 2020), pp. 31–45.

18 Duke-Mosier, 'Drinking the Kool-Aid', p. 33.

19 Jim Jones in High Deaf, 'Jim Jones – Death Tape 1978', *YouTube*, 14 October 2018, https://www.youtube.com/watch?v=ofbGZDbbUsE, 0:18 and 0:38 (accessed 20.7.2022).

20 Jones, 'Jim Jones – Death Tape 1978' (10:01 and 9:56).

21 Jones, 'Jim Jones – Death Tape 1978' (3:54 and 3:59).

22 Jones, 'Jim Jones – Death Tape 1978' (13:54 and 15:47).

23 Jones, 'Jim Jones – Death Tape 1978' (32:37).

24 Jones, 'Jim Jones – Death Tape 1978' (42:31).

25 Duke-Mosier, 'Drinking the Kool-Aid', p. 36.

26 Sean McCloud quoted in Duke-Mosier, 'Drinking the Kool-Aid', p. 34.

27 Duke-Mosier, 'Drinking the Kool-Aid', p. 34.

28 Duke-Mosier, 'Drinking the Kool-Aid', p. 34.

29 Bruce Lincoln in Duke-Mosier, 'Drinking the Kool-Aid', p. 35.

30 David Chidester, *Salvation and Suicide: Jim Jones, the Peoples Temple and Jonestown* (Bloomington, IN: Indiana University Press, 2003), p. 129.

31 Chidester, *Salvation and Suicide*, p. 130.

32 Jim Jones in Chidester, *Salvation and Suicide*, p. 148.

33 Duke-Mosier, 'Drinking the Kool-Aid', p. 37.

34 Jones, 'Jim Jones – Death Tape 1978' (9:27).

35 Jones, 'Jim Jones – Death Tape 1978' (9:31, 9:40 and 9:42).

36 Jones, 'Jim Jones – Death Tape 1978' (13:54 and 14:06).

Conclusion

'How many examples are you going to use in your book, Dr Robinson?' This is a question a student asked me in class a couple of weeks ago. The student continued by naming all of the different ways that they saw theology as being manipulated in historical contexts. 'I don't know if I will have time for all of those,' I responded, 'but they certainly fit the criteria.'

'You could be writing this book for ever!' they exclaimed. 'Yes, yes I could', I replied.

I started thinking about this idea when I was doing my PhD in 2009, as I mentioned in the Introduction. That story is true, and it stirred in me this feeling that I was somehow taking the easy way out by studying peacebuilders in Northern Ireland. It feels now as though I have finally seen 'the other side' of this theological task. In Northern Ireland I studied people who used their theology in order to further the cause of peace in their land. Now I study those who use theology for oppression and violence. I suppose I should have known that this was two sides of the same coin, and that anything that can be used for good can also be used for evil. I have seen *Star Wars* (finally), after all.

I did not know if anyone would be on this journey with me, academically speaking. I famously was called a Marxist in the University of Edinburgh's research seminar when I presented this idea to a group of my peers.[1] But as I kept reading, I began to realize that I was in no way the first person to wrestle with the idea of the human manipulation of theology. Theologians are endlessly discussing and praising those who do theology for the sake of good, and yet only a handful discuss those who are doing theology for the cause of bad.

Practical Theology as a field acknowledges the idea that theology is a human construct, and that's why it serves as my methodology umbrella. We built our entire field of theology around this idea in order to survive the Enlightenment. Theologians like Schleiermacher were so very keen to analyse theology as it was practised in the local congregations. The essential element of Practical Theology is that humans take theological theory and they enact it in the world. I was raised in this academic tradition, and I was taught very early on that the interest in Practical Theology was not in the 'what' but in the 'how' of theology. It is no wonder, then, that I became interested in the subject of bad theology. I was deeply invested in the work of people who were peacebuilders, and how they justified their work based on their own theological views. I spent years writing about this, and even published a book about it: *Embodied Peacebuilding: Reconciliation as Practical Theology*. It seems obvious now that I would peek around the corner at the other side; to see how theology was working towards violence but remained justified in the minds of those who were enacting it in the world. Bad Practical Theology was always going to be written, and since all theology is Practical Theology, I should clarify and say that *Bad Theology: Oppression in the Name of God* was always going to be written. It is the bookend to my first book, and while I would like to take credit for being able to see this far into the future, it was simply a natural progression of the research process (with a lot of support from my husband, friends, family, cats and publisher).

I was concerned that my ideas about bad theology would only reside in the Practical Theology realm. I did not mind that, but I also wanted to open the discussion up to a bigger audience. So I wanted to look through other theological disciplines to try and get their viewpoint on the matter. I was drawn to Kaufman and Tanner in the systematic world; I saw that they too had thoughts about the connection between theology and the social world. Kaufman's ideas about 'reality God' and 'God' were invaluable. Theology might aim to acquire knowledge about God, but we are always just a little out of reach, just a little off the mark, and this is because we are not quite able to access that which is 'reality God'. This can result in good theology and it can result in bad theology. Kaufman's ideas related directly to my criteria that involved reflection on one's theology (or lack thereof) as well as a lack of choice in one's theological beliefs.

I was given Tanner's book on a recommendation from a former colleague at the University of Glasgow. Her incredible understanding of the interplay of theology and culture, and the confidence with which she presents it, confirmed ideas that were floating around in my head. Her understanding of the need to keep a check on any given Christian community (and their claims) fed into my criteria about self-reflection and creating us versus them mentalities. Tanner made me confident in my bad theology ideas, and I thank her for that. Her approach to theology as inevitably influenced by culture was refreshing. She presented it as a given, and that is how I got the confidence to present it as such in this book.

Vardy offered the first real instance of where I saw a book that labelled a religion as 'good' or 'bad'. I immediately jumped on this text because I was aware that this undertaking was going to be difficult with regard to labels. I appreciated enormously the way that Vardy very carefully used these designations, and also how he used his own criteria to navigate this world of good and bad religion. If I was going to designate theology as good or bad I would need criteria of my own. Alongside that, I would need for those criteria to be fluid. I am not a systematic theologian (if you haven't gathered that already) and I don't think theology should just remain set in stone for centuries. Practical Theology has a much more fluid account of theology, and I used my criteria as a jumping-off point for discussions that will take place in the future. Vardy is also careful to say that his criteria are a discussion starter and not a hard-and-fast designation for any given religion. His book was a key guide as I navigated the methods around investigating bad theology.

I came across Duncan Ferguson's book on spirituality by chance. I was teaching a class on 'Spiritual Practices of the

World Religions', and I really needed some help. His book came to me highly recommended, and I dug into it immediately. One of the elements that struck me immediately was how Ferguson was able to differentiate between spirituality that was damaging to people and spirituality that uplifted them. I had it in my head that spirituality in general was a personal force for good. What I began to realize is that Ferguson was warning his readers against this kind of mentality. Ferguson says: 'It struck me that religious faith can be enormously powerful in human experience, lead to health, human flourishing, and social responsibility, but also it can lead to an orientation of fear, zealotry, and intolerance.'² And there it was. Much like my nervous peeks around the corner from peacebuilding theology to violent theology, I got to see the same idea from someone outside of my field of study. Here again was someone who was discussing the good and the bad side of their respective field. I took Ferguson's ideas about flourishing and about justice and equality into the criteria. I thought they were required for good theology – much like life-giving spirituality.

Maybe I was a Marxist, but I certainly wasn't the only one it seems.

When it came to my examples for bad theology, I had no fewer than ten to twelve of them scribbled on a piece of paper. I tried not to think about the criteria too much whenever I listed potential cases because I wanted to see if they would organically fit into the limitations I had created. There were a few I had studied intimately, and others where I got to go into deep research dives. Having researched a great deal about the influence of theology on colonialization in various parts of the world, I knew that I wanted to analyse an area that would reflect that mentality. I also wanted an area that had suffered from violence as a result of this theologically justified colonialization. Unfortunately, there are many to choose from. South Africa was somewhere that I had not written about previously, though I had read a great deal about it. It was an exploration to go through the history of this nation, and to see the bad theology at work. While some snapshots are violent but quick, the bad theology of the Afrikaners was long. Very long. They went from minority to majority, and they took their theology with them. This theology, which started as being community-based, slowly became increasingly political and nationally oppressive. The Afrikaners played the theological long game, and it worked for them.

Leaning into the idea of colonialization, I moved to the UK and the Puritans. I grew up learning about these people who were escaping a land of religious intolerance (as the story goes), but the continuation of their travels gets lost in the mythology of US history. As I was prepping to teach a course on 'Religion in the USA', I came across Winthrop's speech. I was amazed, shocked and horrified by what I read. The use of theology to create a community of people who felt justified in their actions against the native peoples was astounding, and when I read further about the massacre of the native peoples by Mason, it secured this group as one of my examples. The comments about the native peoples in the fire alone was enough to make one shudder. This was an example of bad theology that fizzled out pretty quickly, but what I did take note of here was the way that their bad theology influenced the history of the USA. They had a very clear sense of what would come to be called 'Manifest Destiny'. Their ideas would lead to westward expansion whereby there would be more massacres and more bad theology. So while their community was short lived, their legacy of bad theology is quilted into the very fabric of the USA.

I grew up in the American South, and so the KKK have always been of particular interest to me with regard to their theological beliefs. I have seen their parades, and I have witnessed the hate that they perpetuate in my region of the world. As I analysed their documents (of which there are many) I began to see that they were very interested in showcasing their theological analysis with regard to the human race. Their focus on a divinely ordained hierarchy when it comes to gender, sexuality, nationality and race is convoluted at best. They take stories from the Old Testament and they manipulate them to fit their own narrative. Their bad theology is systematically laid out in their writings. They don't stray from their original message, and they repeat it over and over to their followers until it is ingrained. In some ways, the simplicity of the list of people they hate makes it easier for them to pass down their bad theology from generation to generation. And as the quest for equality in the USA continues to this day, the KKK will seemingly continue to pop up strategically to continue their campaign of theology, intimidation and violence.

And finally, Jim Jones. I must admit that my interest in Jones goes beyond just my desire to pick a cult leader for my book on bad theology. Jones was an ordained minister in my denomination. It felt close to home, even if it was years before I was born. I wanted to understand how this person could go from having a seemingly open and inclusive theology, to then murdering his entire congregation. Jones created such an intense us versus them with his followers that they were willing to travel to another country in order to escape perceived oppression. Meanwhile, Jones would sprinkle in religious rhetoric here or there to keep them participating in his church. Finally, he granted himself God-like status, which solidified his ability to speak as an ultimate authority on theology. However, as we can see from the deaths of his people, he was following an *intensely* bad theology. A murderous, awful, terrible theology.

So why write a book on a topic like this? People ask me this all the time. They ask me because I am a Christian theologian, and because I am an ordained minister. Would it not be easier to write about topics like peacebuilding? Topics that highlight the good that theology is doing in the world as opposed to the bad? On the one hand, I can say that I've already done that, but this wouldn't really hit at the truth of the matter. I have previously written articles and chapters about growing up in the Southern Baptist Church, and how I had great desires to be a minister within that church. But I was repeatedly denied this and forced to move to a different denomination to pursue my ordination. What I don't always talk about is how that move broke my heart. This was the church of Grandmother, and pot luck dinners, and plays about sheep, and choir, and youth group. It was my home.

What I realized is that the same place that brought me so much joy theologically also brought me the utmost pain. One place was able to bring me to uncontrollable laughter and a childhood of fantastic memories, but also bring me to overwhelming tears and feelings of inadequacy. When I would tell people about my experiences, they would feel bad for me, but they were always quick to defend the institution or to defend the theology of that church. They would also move to highlight the happy memories I had in the church. Focus on those, they would always say. This always seemed like half a response to me.

And now I realize why that is. Viewing something that is inherently human as being undeniably good, with no capacity for bad, is very very dangerous. I saw it first-hand in my own way, but others will have stories to add to mine and the examples I have given. To call something out as having the capacity to be bad is not to say the whole thing is bad, but only that the practice of this particular theological belief is oppression in a given context to a given people. Tanner speaks about how we must hold communities responsible for their theological conclusions. If we do not do this, then we will be doomed to continue to write books about bad theology over and over and over.

We cannot hold up institutions comprised of humans as God. And we must certainly not hold up people who say they speak for God as God. We also cannot just label every catastrophe that happens as being the result of theology that is some sort of false religion. However, there are real consequences to not holding bad theology in check. There are horrific stories of the evils of apartheid, the descriptions of burning people and stolen lands, people of colour hanging from trees while others stare at them, and a photo of 900 people laid out side by side in a jungle in Guyana. This list could go on and on. We have just lived through a global pandemic, and all the while there were preachers on the television selling miracle solutions to scientific problems, promising the protection of 'reality God', while their followers put themselves in risky or deadly positions based on this bad theology. These ministers got rich and their followers died. And so it goes.

For now, let us continue this conversation. Let's add more criteria or take some away. Let's keep this conversation going. When we use phrases like 'This can never happen again', let's actually hold to that. As a Practical Theologian, I am not just called upon to say what is happening in the world, but also what *should* be happening in the world. As a result, we need to offer a voice for those who have been oppressed by the very theology that they hold dear. This is not false religion; it is Christianity served by false prophets who profit from bad theology on a daily basis.

And to all those little girls out there who have big dreams to speak one day from the pulpit or the academic podium, we see you.

Notes

1 I should say that only one person called me a Marxist and everyone else actually engaged with the content and was very supportive!

2 Duncan Ferguson, *Exploring the Spirituality of the World Religions* (London: Continuum, 2010), p. viii.